CHALLENGE OF A GENERATION

Beyond the Crash of '87

E. S. Gayed

New York Institute of Finance

LIBRARY OF CONGRESS
Library of Congress Cataloging-in-Publication Data

Gayed, E. S.
    The challenge of a generation : beyond the crash of '87 / by E.S.
Gayed.
        p.   cm.
    Includes index.
    ISBN 0-13-124397-7 : $21.95
    1. United States--Economic conditions--1981- 2. Economic
history--20th century.   I. Title.
HC106.8.G38 1988
330.973'0927--dc19   HC   88-22548
                                     106.8   CIP
                                     G-38
                                     1989

This publication is designed to provide accurate and authoritative information in regard to the subject matter covered. It is sold with the understanding that the publisher and author are not engaged in rendering legal, accounting, or other professional service. If legal advice or other expert assistance is required, the services of a competent professional person should be sought.

From a Declaration of Principles Jointly Adopted by a Committee of the American Bar Association and a Committee of Publishers and Associations

Printed in the United States of America

10 9 8 7 6 5 4 3 2 1

New York Institute of Finance
(NYIF Corp.)
70 Pine Street
New York, New York 10270-0003

To Nadia and Michael, my precious love,
to Ester and Shaker, who gave me birth,
and to Mary and Dr. Albert who blessed me with the
greatest gift of my life.

Perseverance has been the hidden force behind every
success story in the history of mankind and will continue
to be the source of progress for the remainder of man's
life on earth. No matter how bad things get, if you
persevere, chances are that you will conquer all
adversities and prevail.

— The Author

Contents

❑ 2

❑ 3

❑ 4

❏ 7

In Search of Identity, 137

The Postindustrial Society

❏ 8

The Frontiers of Supertechnology, 163

Toward a World of Abundance

❏ 9

The Road to Globalization, 179

❑ **10**

❑ **11**

Introduction

On October 19, 1987, billions of dollars were wiped out. The one-day bear market that hit Wall Street was the most precipitous decline in securities prices ever recorded in history. Investors watched the melting of wealth and the massacre of corporate America with disbelief. Overnight, the sudden and unannounced split in values touched each and every issue listed on all exchanges around the world. Whether it was program trading, portfolio insurance, or otherwise, the damage was swift, painful, and broad based. Although naive pop and mom investors were initially disconcerted, they flocked to brokerage offices seeking to capitalize on the opportunity. Overall, the crash of 1987 spread fear and uncertainty in world markets, stunned people around the globe, and left scared souls behind.

In news reports then, the media chose to dwell upon explanation and analysis of the crash. They neglected to set forth a call to action to prevent the crash from developing further. For this book, we therefore resorted to the files of economic history in search of both an answer and a plan of action. In the twentieth century, a stock market crash had happened only once before: just when the Great Depression was about to take its toll on a whole generation. To those who studied the history of crashes and panics, the crash of 1987 brought to mind the roaring twenties and what followed: the worst calamity in the history of our nation.

The book opens by reliving the economic and sociological environment that led to the Great Depression in the early 1920s. It examines the record of the history of that era, from banking to farming, inflation, and the real estate boom and bust. It also focuses on the stock market bubble and the crash of 1929 as precursors to the Great Depression.

The business environment of the eighties is then studied, with all its promises and discontents. Our final triumph over the inflation of the seventies; the depression that is taking its toll on the agricultural sector; the real estate bonanza; the debt plague at the consumer, corporate, and government levels; and, finally, the crash of 1987 are examined.

Furthermore, the book deliberates on the similarities and differences between the eighties and the twenties. Besides citing differences in demographics and the regulatory, economic, and social makeup of America in the eighties, we point to structural safety nets that have been formulated to prevent the recurrence of the depression. We also present the problems from which our economy is suffering today and offer a menu of options that we can choose from to steer our fortunes to safe shores. In sum, we discuss the reasons behind our declining competitiveness in the world market and the choices available to revitalize our country.

OUR RECENT HISTORY

Real estate has grown at a phenomenal rate in the past few years. Both households and corporations are loaded with debt. The government is incurring a huge deficit. Banks are struggling with the shadow of default of less developed countries (LDCs). What will happen to real estate if we enter a severe recession? How would a recession affect people's net worth? How could it affect our future?

Today, America is blessed with the most skilled labor force on the face of the earth. The baby boomers are at the peak of their productivity. The two-paycheck society that made its debut in the seventies is capable of taking us to new horizons of wealth and new sources of growth. What role can the baby boomers play in the future? Are they going to pay the hefty price of economic poverty in the years ahead?

We live in the era of supertechnology. Wonder drugs, automation, artificial intelligence, and powerful computers hold great promise for the future of mankind. What role will technology play in our future? Can it find an answer to our problems? Can it generate new opportunities and find solutions for the prophecies of doom?

The seventies and eighties witnessed a noticeable deterioration in our industrial base. Several factors contributed to declining productivity. We lost our competitiveness in the world arena. One of the reasons cited was the Japanese invasion of the global market. How did Japan rise to become an economic superpower? What should we do to regain our industrial superiority?

We are told that we are living in a postindustrial society and that the service sector should continue to grow until it replaces manufacturing. Indeed, the service sector has provided jobs to millions of baby boomers entering the job market. However, can the service sector fill the gap left by manufacturing? Should we rely on it to regain our declining standard of living? Can we afford to continue to transfer manufacturing to offshore facilities and still maintain control over our strategic resources?

What can we do to prevent a business slowdown from developing into a total collapse? Does entrepreneurship in America have an answer? What are our options? Is World War III inevitable at the close of this century? Is our generation doomed to helplessness? What can we learn from history and what can we do to secure our future?

Internationally, we witnessed several socialist countries undergoing radical reforms during the eighties. At the top of the list are the leaders of socialism: Russia and China. Are those movements real? What implications will they have on the future? What will happen to those masses on the path of reform if the world falls into a depression? Are we willing to forsake another triumph of capitalism around the world?

WHAT THE EXPERTS SAY

In their analyses of this multifaceted situation, some experts have referred to the widely acclaimed long-term depression wave theory developed by a Russian economist, Nicholai Dimitrievich Kondratieff, at the turn of the century. The Kondratieff prophecy, which predicts a depression every 60 years, has long haunted economists and raised the question of doom in their minds. Are we helpless against nature's laws? Is our future doomed to the inevitable Kondratieff killer wave? In this book, we investigate the tenets of that prophecy of doom and discuss its findings in detail.

Similarly, several new books have predicted that we are about to enter a depression in the 1990s. Can this really happen? What differences exist between the eighties and the twenties? Is our safety net sufficient to prevent such a calamity from taking hold? Is the decline of our dollar in the international market significant to our future? Could we be about to witness an industrial renaissance instead of a bust? More important than answering these pressing questions is to recognize the challenges ahead of us.

THE CHALLENGES WE FACE

First, there is the challenge of an overextended real estate market and a looming slowdown in that vital sector of the economy. In fact, its health or sickness determines the fate of many other industries.

Recapturing our status in the world market is another challenge that we have to address. In order for us to do so, we must formulate strategies to compete with the unstoppable

Japan. In this book, we study the legendary success of the Japanese in order to be in a better position to assess their potential and to develop our comeback strategies. We also investigate the future of international collaboration and the prospects of worldwide changes.

Undoubtedly, our greatest challenge in the years ahead is to regain our past industrial superiority and to revitalize our manufacturing base. We will study the reasons behind our industrial decline and then formulate a plan of action to help us to regain our competitiveness in the world and reverse our declining standard of living.

Finally, we examine the role of technology in creating wealth and future sources of growth. We address the globalization of the world economy and then rethink the promise of capitalism. And we touch upon important developments that hold great hope for the free enterprise system.

This book has no intention of predicting the future or lamenting the past. Instead, we reflect on the possible causes and the remedies that *we the people* could effect. This comprehensive analysis of the most important problems facing our world today presents alternatives that we could choose from to avert a repeat of the thirties.

A SYNTHESIS OF APPROACHES

This book deliberates on trends that evolved in our past, shape our present, and will influence our future in the critical decade ahead of us. It puts old concepts to the test in the context of the present, without drawing the conclusions that unfolded immediately after their development. Trends of long-term dimensions tend to create other trends and to develop into meaningful implications for our lives. Study of these trends can certainly clarify our present and future options.

Many of these trends have been discussed in other studies. The success of the Japanese and the lessons that they brought with them to the international arena have probably been addressed in greater detail in specialized books. Globalization has also been elaborated upon in reams of articles in the *Harvard Business Review,* in *Business Week,* in *Forbes,* and in *Fortune.* Likewise, capitalism and socialism as ideologies were commonly studied as part of our education, and technology has always been a most thrilling subject to our imagination.

In sum, all these interesting and intertwined topics deserve a much more elaborate discussion than this book could possibly allow for. Yet, only when we bring those thoughts together can major trends and intertrends be visualized as converging toward meaningful conclusions.

❑ 1

To Hell and Back

Echoes of the Roaring Twenties

"We in America today are nearer to the final triumph over poverty than ever before in the history of any land. The poorhouse is vanishing from among us. We have not yet reached the goal, but, given the chance to go forward with the policies of the last eight years, we shall soon, with the help of God, be in sight of the day when poverty will be banished from this nation."

President Herbert Hoover, 1928

In the history of America, two great events had more far-reaching consequences than any others: the Civil War and the Great Depression. While the former established the free enterprise system as the dominant economic practice in the United States, the painful experience of the Great Depression led to government intervention that did away with laissez-faire capitalism.

Indeed, October 29, 1929, Black Tuesday, was a day of infamy in the history of the free enterprise system. It witnessed the stock market crash and signalled the onset of the Great Depression, which lasted over a decade. Some called it "the day when the bubble burst," while others spent their lives haunted by its consequences. What led to that calamity? Could it have been predicted before? What were the signs of the time that could have warned about the forthcoming ordeal? Let us go back to those days, long gone, and relive the makeup of a crisis.

LA BELLE EPOQUE

At the turn of the century, the world was a happy capitalist system. Those early years were known as *la belle epoque*—the good era. Europe was ruled by a single family of kings, and the gap was very wide between the haves and have-nots. There were no taxes in those days, and wealth was concentrated in the hands of a few. At that time, one-third of the labor force worked in agriculture, and half the population lived on farms. The 1910s witnessed the transformation of an agrarian society into an industrial one.

The world was entering a century of mature ideologies and gigantic leaps in business, technology, entertainment, medicine, politics, and all other endeavors of life. Revolution after revolution faced mankind in the decades to follow and these first few years paved the way for great events in the history of America. The United States was about to enter the decade of the "greats": the great victory of World War I, the great industrial boom, the commercialization of the great automobile, the discovery of the great radio, the heydays of the movie greats, the great land boom, the great bull market, the great crash, the Great Depression, and the great transition of world leadership from the United Kingdom to the United States.

An early precursor to some of these revolutions occurred in the financial sector, which was shaken in 1907 by a banking mini-war that claimed the Knickerbocker Trust Co., then the third largest bank in New York, as its first victim. Because this loss did not extend to the entire nation, the panic of those days became known as "the rich man's panic." Yet, it turned the attention of the administrators to the fragility of the banking establishment. Congress, alarmed by a shaken financial system, appointed the National Monetary Commission to study the state of the banking industry. This study recognized that an institution was needed to take charge of the financial structure and act as the ultimate support during banking panics. The investigation finally led to the passage of the Federal

Reserve Act and the establishment of the Federal Reserve Board (FED) in 1913.

At the beginning, the FED's role was to ensure the soundness of the banking system so that temporary dislocations could be contained. Banks loaned money to brokers, farmers, businessmen, and homeowners. At times of money shortages or excessive demand for loans, the FED acted as the bankers' bank and provided them with liquidity. Over the years, the FED's responsibilities expanded to include controlling the flow of money and balancing inflation and unemployment on a growing economic course.

THE EVIL OF WARS

World War I was declared in August 1914. A mini-panic developed and the stock market plummeted. The New York Stock Exchange closed from August through November. However, shortly thereafter, war orders from Europe flooded the country; the "Guns of August" gave a tremendous boost to the steel and oil industries. The shipbuilding industry was also in its heyday and prospered from the transportation of goods between Europe and North America. All this triggered a healthy economic recovery and gave a huge stimulus to business in America. New records were achieved in agriculture, industry, and commerce.

On January 24, 1916, the Supreme Court ruled that federal income tax was constitutional. In that same year, taxes were doubled from 1 percent to 2 percent on income above the $3,000 exemption limit. And for the first time, the United States soared to become the largest creditor nation in the world. In response to demand, the government embarked on expansionary policies to finance the war. Government Liberty Bonds were issued. The U.S. government made loans to the Allies in an effort to help rebuild chaotic European finances. As a result, money in circulation and bank credits expanded rapidly.

Wars are notorious for infusing inflation into the economy, and inflation grew rampant under the impact of the rising demand for consumption. Soon, the phenomenon spread throughout the industrial nations. Germany led the way, as prices rose at 14,000 percent by 1923. A barter society threatened the existence of the reichsmark, which was pegged to gold by 1924. The inability of the incumbent German administration to control inflation was cited as one of the major factors that helped Hitler rise to power.

That surge in inflation at the close of the 1910s and into the 1920s compelled the world to adopt the gold standard. Those years witnessed the wildest fever of speculation in gold and precious metals ever. As inflation zoomed upward, the FED was quick to assume its responsibility and tightened the monetary reins. In early 1920, the rates charged by banks on

Figure 1–1. *Inflation in the 1920s*

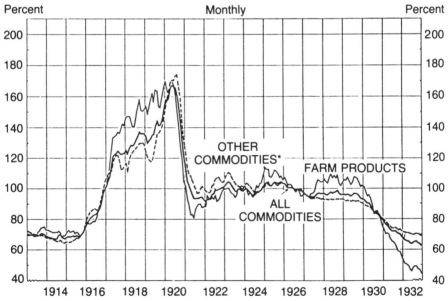

Source: Federal Reserve Board.

short-term loans exceeded 7 percent. Long-term bonds yielded slightly more than 5.5 percent. As the cost of borrowing money increased, it put a dent in commodities' price advances. Soon enough, inflation subsided by late 1921.

Generally, inflation cannot be brought under control without the pain and anguish of high unemployment, serious business contraction, depressed corporate profits, and widespread bankruptcies. In the early twenties, as an era of hyperinflation was about to end and not return for the next 60 years, the misfortunes of the farmers were about to begin.

ON THE OTHER SIDE OF PARADISE

When wars erupt among nations, economies are pressed for excessive demand that the existing production capacity cannot meet. Until production facilities expand, prices tend to move up and inflation rises. Since the agricultural sector is very sensitive to inflationary forces, prices of farm products soared above 200 percent by 1919. With it, real estate values of farmlands appreciated 150 percent from 1915 to 1919. From 1916 to 1922, mortgage debt on farmlands escalated at a phenomenal rate of 235 percent. Inflation, with its usual illusory promise of richness, encouraged farmers to extend beyond their means.

History has shown that good times are followed by painful adjustments and that inflation is followed by deflation. Inflation encourages people to borrow now and pay later with cheaper dollars. The farmers of the 1910s were no different; as prices kept rising, so did their debts. Then came the time when the trend reversed; deflation wiped out debt as well as wealth, and persistent declines in commodity prices affected both lenders and borrowers.

The sharp rise in real interest rates in the early 1920s caused a plummet in commodity prices, and farmers were the first to feel the squeeze of deflation. Asset values, net worth, and borrowing power evaporated. Much of that wealth was

Figure 1–2. Agriculture in the 1920s

MORTGAGE DEBT AND REAL ESTATE VALUES
1912–1914 = 100

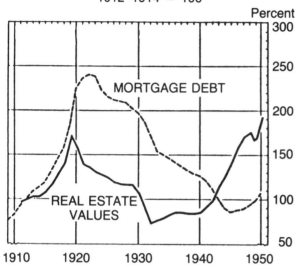

Source: Federal Reserve Board.

only paper profits born of the inflation of World War I. But those sweet dreams of prosperity quickly disappeared.

In 1921, agriculture went into a depression of its own. Bankruptcies of farms became commonplace. Conditions in the farming industry worsened and claimed the fortunes of hundreds of small farmers. It took two decades to liquidate the debt accumulated in that vital sector of the economy. In addition, many banks that had lent money to farmers during the inflationary years felt the sour taste of default and incurred staggering losses.

During the twenties and well into the thirties, agriculture suffered from declining prices and falling demand. Farmers missed the go-go years that began on Wall Street in the twenties. They experienced a severe depression when the rest of the world around them enjoyed an era of great prosperity. They sought help from the government, but their pleas fell on deaf ears. The value of their land was adversely affected by the decline in commodity prices, and their debts became a heavy burden that declining profits could not support. They were simply living on the other side of paradise. The miseries of the farmers sounded an unheeded warning of the evils of deflation.

THE RIVIERA OF AMERICA

Then, the roaring twenties began. The years of inflation were not yet gone—at least in the minds of land speculators. For them, it was the time for real assets to appreciate. The invisible hand chose Florida as the next step in the speculative mania that erupted. The southwestern region of Florida suddenly witnessed the greatest land price boom of the time, probably due to the mild climate of Miami Beach and Coral Gables.

A world of make believe and a house of cards were being built around the hopes of those seeking to get rich quick in what seemed to be an endless rise in real estate prices. The fact that Florida was swampland did not discourage those who never intended to live there. Unfortunately, greed is infinitely more potent than fear, and as the constant new supply of buyers kept coming to Florida, voices of conservatism were ridiculed. The gambling instinct convinced the masses that somehow the miraculous stroke of blind fortune was in Florida. The real estate mania had the ultimate touch of seduction as options on land were sold. Newcomers had to pay only a token amount to preserve their right to buy properties at a fixed price, hoping that at a later date they would sell the right at a hefty profit.

From 1921 to 1926, construction contracts soared. Mortgage borrowing added further strains on the ballooning household debt that increased from approximately $130 billion to more than $190 billion—over a 50 percent rise in less than six years. The cumulative debt that characterized the period was little noticed by the banks and the administrators.

The housing market, as we all know, constitutes the backbone of several other industrial sectors. Its slowdown at the close of the twenties precipitated the decline of the economy. At the onset of the depression, consumers were loaded with debt. When unemployment started to rise, they were strapped and could not meet their obligations. Meanwhile, banks, which had financed the speculative mania, found themselves burdened with questionable loans.

Debt resulting from real estate speculation added to the economic illiquidity. As the end of the decade approached, both the agricultural and housing markets were undergoing a serious contraction: Farmers were bankrupt and real estate owners were highly leveraged.

Real estate was not the only speculative mania of the twenties. From 1922 to 1929, another bubble was in the making: the stock market, which was about to bring the economy to its moment of truth.

THE EARLY DAYS OF A RISING GIANT

The early part of the twentieth century witnessed an era of great discoveries. The industrial revolution was progressing on a course that was to shape the history of mankind. The Wright brothers were dreaming of their flying machines and were about to bring the world closer together. Electricity was still in its infancy, and the atom was not yet discovered. Agriculture was being steadily replaced by industry and was in the process of integrating vertically to provide more efficient means of conquering famines and food shortages. America was the land that offered the ultimate dream to immigrants from around the globe. Capitalism was just about to move from its raw form to what we know it to be today.

The 1920s was a decade of ambitious aspirations and abundant prosperity. The industrial revolution was shifting gears and promised the world a higher standard of living. The new discoveries and innovations of the time stimulated business in every sector of the economy and created wealth for the rising giant. Man was about to get used to the new horseless carriage, the automobile. It was the time to pave roads and build gasoline stations and refineries. The automobile industry fueled demand for glass, steel, leather, and rubber. The coal, machine tool, and clothing industries were also expanding at a fast pace. Technology in those days was a source of new jobs and increasing prosperity. The radio broke the monotony of silent life, and the movie business, searching for identity, was about to deliver an abundance of movie greats. Electric power, a prewar innovation, doubled in its generating capacity. The great agrarian society of the past was being transformed into the wealthy industrial society of the future. Cities were built and existing ones were expanded as the children of farmers sought their places in the great new manufacturing society.

THE WOBBLING BANKS

The state of the banks was both the cause and consequence of the fragile economic environment that led to the depression. During the 1910s and the early 1920s, banks exhausted a good part of their liquidity extending loans to finance World War I, and to finance the explosive and speculative appreciation of farmland prices and the real estate mania in Miami and other parts of the country.

Real interest rates remained high following the collapse in commodity prices. While the economy, as represented by industrial production, grew moderately, banks continued to expand their credit. As the agricultural sector faltered and the real estate bubble was punctured, loan default claimed several banks as its casualties. The number of banks started to shrink.

In a desperate move to recoup some of those losses and questionable outstanding loans, banks sought refuge in the lucrative equities market. Indeed, the stock market was about to embark on its best days ever. The higher the stock market rose, the more credit was channelled into margin buying. Policies adopted by the FED to stabilize financial markets prompted rapid credit inflation and fueled the rise of financial

Figure 1–3. The Day the Banks Closed

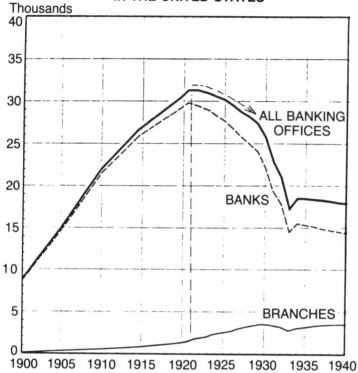

ALL COMMERCIAL BANKING OFFICES IN THE UNITED STATES

Source: Federal Reserve Board.

assets. More and more banks increased their leverage expo-
sure and plunged into the lucrative high-return market.
However, more leverage implied greater risk. The result was
a narrowing of spreads between high- and low-quality debt.
The banks' traditional revenue-producing avenues, corporate
and consumer lending, shifted to financial markets. Lending
strategies changed course from financing real asset acquisitions to fueling financial asset speculation.

The severe dislocation of banks' asset allocations played
an important role in destabilizing investments and chan-
nelling resources to nonproductive ends. The illiquidity crisis
was further exacerbated by the rising margin debt. Despite the

vulnerable position of the banking system, the real panic that developed in the 1930s was propelled by the gloomy psychology that developed after the crash of 1929.

A RENDEZVOUS WITH FATE

Speculation, which characterized those years of excesses, soon moved to Wall Street. It started gradually after the recession of 1921–22. The Railroad Bond Index led the way after several years in the doldrums. Interest rates were on the decline, and the appealing returns on bonds attracted investors.

During the summer of 1921, the stock market began its climb from around the 65 mark on the Dow Jones Index. At that time, no one could have foreseen its final peak; it would have sounded insane to predict that the rise would carry the Dow Jones Industrial Average 600 percent in the following eight years. By early 1923, the Dow moved decisively above the 100 mark—the upper range for the peak of cycles that occurred during the previous ten years. A period of sideways consolidation followed, but, by the summer of 1924, the market was ready to resume its advance. The Dow Jones Industrial Average doubled in two years. For the better part of 1926, the Dow stood at 180.

The appeal of financial assets as a vehicle for investment was overshadowed in its early stages by the lucrative real estate market. However, between 1924 and 1926, the rate of return on equities far outpaced the appreciation of real estate values. Investors were more attracted to the stock market, which represented the new promise of wealth. On August 2, 1926, Thomas Cochrane, partner at the J. P. Morgan Company, said, "General business throughout the country is fine, and it should continue so indefinitely." Although the market had a short period of consolidation for the rest of 1926, that was only in preparation for the most sensational advance in market history.

The public was also watching the fabulous rise in stock prices and recognized its superior appreciation potential. But it still needed assurance from the experts to commit its investments to that lucrative market. Indeed, numerous experts generously offered their optimistic predictions of the great era that the economy had entered. They cited the rise and quality of future earnings and spoke highly of the breakthrough inventions of Radio Corporation of America, the robust earnings of General Motors, and the genius of Henry Ford, a living legend.

The market itself reassured any remaining skeptics as it proceeded with its historic advance in 1927. Fortunes were being made in a hurry. With every passing day, a millionaire was born in Detroit, Chicago, Wilmington, New York City, and every leading metropolis where speculators breathed stocks. It was a great time for investment trusts, the old name for mutual funds. People came to the market in abundance, with promises of wealth that went far beyond the dreams of avarice. Since it was a great time to raise money and go public, the number of secondary and new stock offerings swelled.

By the end of 1927, the market broke through the historic 200-point level. In 1928, it proceeded on its course to exceed 260. Resisting the temptation of jumping into the market was next to an act of insanity. Margin debt exploded to unprecedented levels. Banks, brokerage firms, insurance companies, and publicly held corporations were involved to the hilt, yet the economy was growing at a sluggish rate. Those who were warning of disaster were ridiculed, although the end was near.

THE SLIDE OF THE CENTURY

Then came 1929, a year of big hopes and gloomy prophecies. In January, the market advanced 7 percent and brokers' loans reached $6.7 billion. Industrial production, steel output, automobile manufacturing, and cotton consumption all advanced. New securities issued exceeded $1 billion.

Bethlehem Steel resumed its dividends payout after a five-year lapse. AT&T moved to new highs at $220 per share.

The great bull market continued its feverish rise. Mergers and acquisitions grew. Margin debt continued to grow until it reached unsustainable highs, above $8 billion. New issues kept coming to the market at a rate close to $1 billion per month. The speculative fever was rampant, and the fascinating equities rise on Wall Street had by now attracted the trained nurse, the cab driver, and even the shoe shiner. General Electric reached $396, AT&T sold as high as $304 at its ultimate peak, United States Steel rose to $260, Allied Chemical bettered $350, American Can advanced above $180, Chrysler touched $140, and Radio Corporation of America, later known as RCA, rose to an unprecedented $505. No business was more attractive than making a killing in the stock market. The candy store was wide open for everybody to participate in.

September 3, 1929, witnessed the culmination of the advance: The Dow Jones Industrial Average reached its ultimate peak at 381.17, 123 percent above its previous record at the end of 1926. New issues approximated $1.6 billion, more than any other month on record. The following paragraph from the "Broad Street Gossip" of *The Wall Street Journal* of September 20, 1929, can enlighten us on the psychology of the time:

The news of the day has been big financially and promises to get bigger. We read one day of the formation of a $100,000,000 investment trust, and the next day rumors have it that a $1,000,000,000 investment trust is in the course of formation. Newspaper headlines during the last day or two said that a great oil merger was in the making and that a large steel merger was under way with prospects of another very big consolidation in the same line. Loree is planning a merger of 17 eastern railroads, and there is to be an alliance of some sort between General Motors and Radio. There has been talk of bank mergers, chemical company mergers, gas mergers, power mergers, aviation mergers, food company mergers and asbes-

Figure 1–4. The Perils of Margin

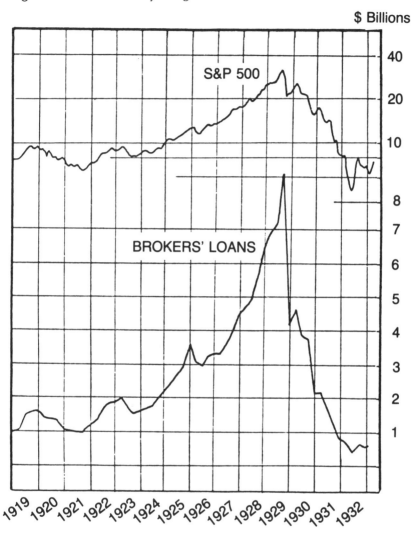

Source: Federal Reserve Board.

tos-gypsum mergers. All of which involves billions of dollars. While things like this are going on one could hardly expect a bear market.

Indeed, the stage was set for the bloodbath to begin. The stock market was on a collision course with fate.

Then came October 1929, which has entered history. On October 1, the president of the American Bankers Association sounded a grave alarm during the annual convention. He warned that there are limits beyond which credit must not be allowed to expand. The stock market decline started with a 19.5-point drop on October 3 and proceeded on an unrelenting downward path. The downturn precipitated in the latter half of the month. On October 23, the market plummeted 31 points, its worst decline in history at that time, on hectic volume amounting to 6,374,960 shares. Bankers issued a reassuring statement on October 24. The stock exchange deferred action on suspension of trading on October 25. Hoover said that the economy was sound. Business leaders reassured the nation with favorable reports. However, panic broke out on Monday, October 28, when the market tumbled 49 points on volume of 9,212,000 shares; the tape was late by 167 minutes.

October 29 was the free fall's most severe drop for the month, with a huge intraday decline of about 70 points. At the close of the day, the industrial average recovered about 41 points. Volume was the heaviest on record, standing at 16,410,000 shares. New York City postponed $60 million in bond offerings, and banks lowered margin requirements from 50 percent to 25 percent. The lowest point the Dow Jones Industrial Average reached on that day was close to 200.

For the month of October 1929, the market lost 39 percent from October's high and 41 percent from September's high. Margin debt fell by $2.44 billion, a reduction of 28 percent from its peak. Industrial production, steel, automobile, and car freight loading all suffered sizable declines. The discount rate was lowered from 6 percent to 5 percent; the brokers' loan rate followed suit and declined from 10 percent to 5 percent.

The market continued to rebound until April 1930, moving back to the 290 mark. For the next two years, the stock market resumed its gradual decline. When it reached its lows in 1932, the Dow Jones Industrial Average stood at around 40. From the crash of October 1929 to its final bottom, the Dow had lost almost 90 percent of its value.

The melting of wealth caused by the crash of 1929 and the devastating decline of security prices signalled the culmination of the pockets of speculation that had swept that decade. Industrial production started on a downward course ahead of the stock market plummet. A reliable barometer of future economic conditions, the market's discounting mechanism predicted the calamity that was shortly to follow.

During the early stages of the depression, there was a complete refusal to face the facts. The days of prosperity that preceded the crash left behind a universe of dreamers. No one wanted to believe that the world of plenty was about to fail on its promises. Neither the administrators nor the public could perceive how deep the depression was going to be. Innocent optimism was ingrained in the minds of a generation that had forgotten the sour lessons of the past. The children of prosperity were still living in their dream world. The stage was, indeed, set for the greatest ordeal of the century.

WHAT IS A DEPRESSION?

A depression is a very severe contraction of business activities. It differs from a recession in both the depth and duration of its impact on all sectors of the economy. On average, post-World War II recessions lasted between 9 and 12 months and were accompanied by a decline of 2 percent to 3 percent in real Gross National Product (GNP). On the other hand, the Great Depression of 1929–1933 lasted for over 3 1/2 years and caused serious disruption in the job market. During the entire 1930s, unemployment remained consistently above 14 percent. At the trough of the depression, 25 percent of the working population was out of work. Of 52 million

Americans in the labor force, 13 million lost their jobs. Bread lines and the gray armies of job seekers became the symbols of that period of our economic history.

The depression started around August 1929, when unemployment was a scant 3.2 percent. The collapse of the economy continued on its course until March 1933. Real GNP plummeted by over 33 percent, and industrial production declined by 50 percent. World trade shrank to one-third of its value—from $33 billion in 1928 to $13 billion in 1932. Over the course of four years, from 1929 to 1933, gross private domestic investment plummeted from $16 billion to less than $1 billion. The M1 money supply, narrowly defined as currency in circulation plus demand deposits, declined by 27 percent, and M2, which is M1 plus time deposits, was cut by 33 percent during the same four years.

Wholesale prices declined a hefty 31 percent and the Consumer Price Index (CPI) tumbled by 25 percent during the years that followed the crash of 1929. More than 11,000 banks closed their doors. Total bank deposits plummeted from $49 billion in 1929 to $31 billion in 1933. Over 9 million savings accounts were lost. The bankruptcy rate soared to 85,000 busi-

Figure 1–5. Industrial Production

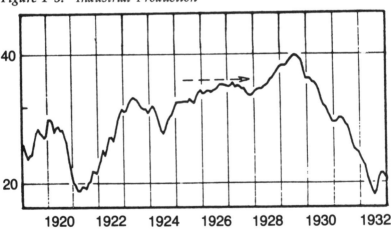

Source: Federal Reserve Board.

nesses. All internationally traded goods plummeted in price under the pressure of deflation.

From March 1933 to May 1937, the economy recovered from that historic contraction. However, it soon fell back into another slump. Full employment was never reached during the thirties. In fact, unemployment fell for a very short period of time to 11 percent, but soon soared again and remained above 14 percent for the rest of the decade.

A secondary depression developed from May 1937 to June 1938. The real GNP receded by 13 percent, and industrial production fell by 32 percent. In 1938, unemployment reached 20 percent of the labor force.

The cumulative collapse that lasted for the balance of the decade wiped out assets, liabilities, and purchasing power. The economy was starved for spending. From 1929 to 1933, the FED kept real interest rates high. AAA bonds yielded close to 14 percent in real terms. In 1931–1932, three-month treasury bills yielded real rates close to 10 percent.

President Roosevelt had little faith in the fiscal stimulus that budget deficits produce. This hesitation to reinflate the economy and to inject badly needed liquidity into the system retarded its recovery. Most European nations, which also fell into a severe depression, recovered by the end of 1932. For all purposes, it was World War II—and the massive government spending that accompanied it—that ended the miseries of the Great Depression.

Describing the aftermath of the depression in a paper submitted to Congress in 1978, Dr. Gottfried Haberler, professor of international trade emeritus at Harvard University, said:

The Great Depression of the 1930s was a world shaking event. For the world economy and economic policy it was a watershed. It gave rise to the Keynesian revolution and shook the confidence in the free market–capitalist economy. It led to far-reaching government intervention in the West. It gave a tremendous boost to the communist system of the East, which seemed to be impervious to the economic disaster that had engulfed the Western World. The economic depression had enormous political repercussions. It helped Hitler come to power and gave him the opportunity for great economic successes, which he effectively used to prepare for World War II, which he unleashed in 1939; it made the Soviet system and Stalin's dictatorship respectable in the West; and it strengthened the militarist regime in Japan.

WHEN REASON FAILS ... BEGGAR THY NEIGHBOR

History shows us that when the pie is large and optimism is overwhelming, people allow others to share in their prosperity. But when the going gets tough and belts have to be tightened, tolerance becomes scant. This truism dominated the international trade scene in the thirties. On June 17, 1930, the Smoot-Hawley trade bill became law. Effective rates of tariffs rose by almost 50 percent on all imported goods. International markets had to bear the brunt of the strongest protectionist act in history.

The passage of that bill triggered a trade war among nations, and retaliation was swiftly felt. Switzerland boycotted U.S. exports, and Italy retaliated with high tariffs on automobiles in June 1930. In August 1932, Canada raised its tariffs threefold on all imports. Spain, Australia, France, Mexico, Cuba, New Zealand, and several other countries engaged in a vicious multilateral trade war. International trade was dealt a severe blow.

Foreign exchange controls were imposed as nations fought any currency appreciation, fearing that this would increase the price of their goods in the world market. The price of gold went from $20.67 to $35 per ounce in an effort to raise prices, fight deflation, and stimulate the economy. Britain went off the gold standard in 1931 and followed with a stiff import tariff early in 1932. Nations refused to lend to each other, and protectionism was rampant. Deflation exacerbated, and unemployment soared worldwide—leading to further shrinking of consumption demand.

These policies became known in economic history books as "beggar thy neighbor" policies. Those restrictive measures resulted in a plummet in the volume of international trade. All countries suffered from idle productive capacity, and the accumulation of inventories in all industrial sectors precipitated a slide in commodity prices. As deflation gathered momentum, it provoked further weakness in the economy. This, in turn, intensified the debt liquidation process and deepened the depression.

Some experts attributed the severity of the depression to the Smoot-Hawley Act. This protectionist bill led to a worldwide decline in demand for both agricultural and manufactured goods. Measured by exports, world trade fell from $33 billion to $13 billion. In fact, the Smoot-Hawley bill was signed by Congress at the onset of the worst economic decline of the century. In retrospect, it seems as if all the wrong things had to happen at the same time to propel the great economic catastrophe to completion. The speculative bubble in real estate, the mania in the stock market, the hesitation of the FED to loosen up the monetary reins, and the worst protectionist bill could not have occurred at a worse time.

To disallow repetition of the beggar thy neighbor policies, the world finally drew up the General Agreement on Tariffs and Trade (GATT). This agreement supported free trade, encouraged liberalization of the exchange of goods and products, and reduced tariffs.

A HOLOCAUST IN THE BANKING SYSTEM

One of the most horrifying episodes in the financial history of the United States was the closing of all the banks in March 1933. Many factors were cited as causes of the banking crisis that began at the close of the twenties and reached disastrous proportions in the early thirties.

Some observers thought that the deflation of the time had played an important role. Others blamed the reluctance of the FED to move decisively when the problem was still benign. Yet others attributed the banking crisis to the British pound being taken off the gold standard. Advocates of free trade accused the Smoot-Hawley protectionist bill of causing shock waves in international financial markets and leading to retaliatory measures from foreign countries, which imposed severe pressure on the banking system and led to devaluation of the dollar. Economists of the time pinpointed the precipitous slide in securities prices combined with exorbitant margin liquidation, which exacerbated risks in the financial sector. As business deteriorated to severe extremes, loan defaults reached astronomical proportions. Despite all of these theories, nearly all observers agreed that the public's reaction was the most important factor that led to a total panic.

At the onset of the Great Depression in the fall of 1929, there were about 24,500 commercial banks, with deposits amounting to some $49 billion. The first wave of runs on banks followed the stock market plummet. Industrial production led the crash and posted a decline during the summer. Margin debt at the peak of the market advance amounted to a hefty $8 billion. Payment of loans became much more difficult after the slide. Depositors became worried and rushed to convert their deposits into cash, which, in turn, led to difficulties that banks were not structured to handle. But the crisis was not yet widespread, and only 659 banks were suspended. In 1930, the number of banks going bankrupt doubled to 1,352.

When the British pound was taken off the gold standard in 1931, doubts were also raised about the soundness of the dollar. International financial relations collapsed, and payments in gold soared to over $725 million. Those uncertainties prompted depositors to withdraw some $6 billion from their bank accounts. At the end of that year, only 19,000 banks with total deposits of $40 billion remained open.

In 1932, the nation's business was in a state of chaos. The economy was in a free fall, and the banking panic reached its worst stage since the late twenties. When a rumor spread about the possibility of devaluation of the dollar, the banking drain intensified. At the close of that year, 18,000 banks were still open with $36 billion in deposits.

Figure 1–6. *Banks in the 1920s*

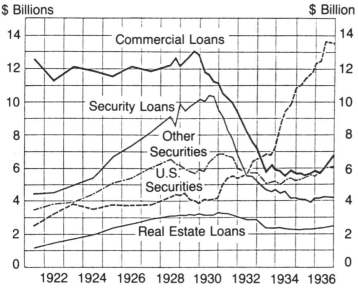

LOANS AND INVESTMENTS OF MEMBER BANKS
(June 30 Through 1928: Call Dates Thereafter)

Source: Federal Reserve Board.

After the defeat of Hoover in the November 1932 election and until Roosevelt's inauguration in March 1933, the nation lacked decisive leadership to reassure depositors of the soundness of the financial system. Panic started in the banks in Michigan during February 1933 and spread to the New York City banks until a "bank holiday" was announced on March 4, 1933. Banks reopened over the span of three days between March 13 and 15. By April 12, only 12,817 banks were open, with deposits slightly exceeding $31 billion.*

---

*The banking panic during the thirties is well documented by Arthur A. Ballantine, Undersecretary of the Treasury from the last years of the Hoover administration through the first months of the Roosevelt administration, in an article entitled "When All The Banks Closed," published in the *Harvard Business Review* in March 1948.

THE NEW DEAL

In August 1932, during the Democratic National Convention and at the depth of the depression, Franklin Delano Roosevelt promised the American people the "New Deal." Major government reforms were proposed to Congress during the famous First Hundred Days of FDR's presidency. Several relief programs were initiated to restructure American institutions.

One of the major results of the depression was increased government involvement in the business sector. The heydays of capitalism came to a sudden jolt as devastating repercussions introduced distrust in market forces. The days of big government's involvement in the free enterprise system were just about to begin. The years following the depression witnessed the birth of regulation and bureaucracy in America that were to prosper and grow for the next several decades. While the Civil War established free enterprise capitalism as the dominant economic form, the depression opened the door for government intervention and regulation.

During the New Deal, the Agricultural Adjustment Act (AAA) was enacted to award subsidies to farmers who limited their crops. The National Industrial Recovery Act (NIRA) allowed industries to form cartels to limit output, fix prices, and thereby counteract the pressures of deflation. NIRA was later deemed unconstitutional and abolished by the Supreme Court in 1935, due to abuse by big producers. In 1934, the Securities Exchange Act gave authority to the FED to limit margin and established the Securities and Exchange Commission (SEC) to police Wall Street. The Social Security System was adopted in 1935. A minimum wage and the 40-hour workweek were established in 1938. The Federal Deposit Insurance Corporation (FDIC) was chartered in 1934 to insure bank deposits.

Roosevelt's New Deal policy was basically targeted at sustaining the lives of the masses of unemployed countrymen. The AAA and NIRA, cornerstones of the New Deal, aimed at restoring prosperity through a redistribution of income in a more equitable manner—into the hands of farmers and workers. Roosevelt believed that structural measures would raise prices and income, put more money into people's hands, and then stimulate consumption. However, the economy responded more to the spirit of leadership that Roosevelt exhibited than to the policies adopted during those postdepression years.

During the 1930s, the voice of John Maynard Keynes, who advocated government spending and expansionary fiscal policies, rose. He believed that during phases of economic deflation, monetary policies may not inject enough liquidity. Therefore, he advocated massive government spending to counteract the pressures imposed on the economy by collapsing commodity prices. However, Roosevelt was not in favor of accommodating the economy through big government spending. Economists and historians cited the mobilization of economic resources for war at the end of the 1930s as the most important factor saving the country from the economic malaise of that decade. As a matter of fact, it was not until 1941 that the GNP surpassed its 1929 level. The mammoth government spending for World War II pulled the country out of the depression. That was the ultimate vindication of Keynes' belief in the power of fiscal policy.

In a speech at the sixteenth Per Jacobsson Lecture in Belgrade, Yugoslavia, on September 30, 1979, Dr. Arthur F. Burns, who was chairman of the Board of Governors of the FED from 1970 to 1978, said:

The breakdown of economic order during the Great Depression was unprecedented in its scale and scope, and it strained the percept of self-reliance beyond the breaking point. With one quarter of the labor force unemployed, personal courage and moral stamina could guarantee neither a job nor a livelihood. Succor finally came through a political idea that was novel to a majority of the American people but compelling nonetheless—namely, that the federal government had a far larger responsibility in the economic sphere than it had hitherto assumed.

WHO'S TO BLAME?

Historians differ in their views of the roots of the problems that eventually led to the total collapse of the 1930s. Some attributed the crash to a stringent monetary policy that the FED adopted in the process of curbing speculation in the stock market. Others, led by faithful followers of the Keynesian school, cited insufficient fiscal stimulus, which the government could have injected to save the economy and release the pressure of the debt liquidation process. Yet others think that the protectionism mandated by the Smoot-Hawley bill led to a sudden shrinking of international trade and flow of funds. At the root of all those explanations, however, lay the inability of the system to understand the consequences of extended and highly leveraged credit markets and their painful unwinding as the debt liquidation process began in earnest.

Neither President Hoover nor his predecessor President Coolidge could see the seeds of the depression in the making during their administrations. Man was still experimenting with modern economics. The greatest intellects of the time missed the signs that were pointing to the inevitable devastation. There was neither a guide nor a parallel from the past with which to compare those times. It was seemingly a brand-new experience in the history of human adversities to which even the most astute fell prey.

For all we know, historians who condemned Hoover, Coolidge, or the FED may have not done anything different if they had been in charge then. The learning curve of nations has, over the course of history, proven to command a high cost. From the Egyptian pharaohs to the Ottoman Empire, the heydays of Alexander the Great, and the mighty Roman Empire, the seeds of destruction were sown for the sage to detect. Yet empires and kingdoms came and went, leaving behind an ever-greener experience to be transferred to future generations.

While Harding, Coolidge, and Hoover thought they brought affluence to Main Street America, nature's laws prevailed. Indeed, the exuberant success of people's fortunes sometimes holds within its progression the seeds of regret. What happened earlier in this century paved the way for an even greater United States to rise from distress and lead the world toward new innovative horizons and breathtaking discoveries. For those who blame the Republicans, let us remind them that no political party ever had a patent on prosperity or disaster. Disaster struck because the environment was ripe for it. The cumulative effects of years of fast growth brought about an episode of adjustment.

OF DASHED DREAMS AND ALLEYS OF DESPAIR

The collapse of the 1930s violently awakened people to their vulnerability to painful economic calamities and shattered their perception of a risk-free world. They became more conservative and less demanding; surviving bad times became their main focus. They valued security after tasting the sour agonies of unemployment and need. They resorted to religion and the warmth of family gatherings. Youngsters learned to respect their elders. The divorce rate fell, and human relations strengthened. Expectations from life were tamed, and people became more cooperative. Adversity helped create a generation of survivors out of yesteryear's preppies. A deepening sense of principles and human values emerged.

As the depression progressed on its course, hostility began to build toward capitalism. The more active presence of government became much more palatable. However, despite the people's shaken confidence in pure capitalism, they never formed a labor party or supported socialism. But the cruelty of the episode gave room to anti-Semitism. The Republicans were condemned for their policies, and the Democrats became people's allies. While President Coolidge escaped the accusation of bringing about the depression, his successor, President Herbert Hoover, was not as lucky.

The younger ones of that generation of survivors carried the lesson of the depression to work. They became conservative leaders whose decisions were based on prudence. Despite all that has been said about the sad ordeal, its occurrence left behind a solid generation that was to bring the country to the forefront of world leadership. They built the America that we know today and left their children a much better life and the highest standard of living on the globe.

THE GREAT TRANSITION

During the turbulent decades of the 1920s and 1930s, the evils of the Great Depression brought an even greater transition: a transition of world leadership and power. A change in command took place: The United States emerged as the center of the West while the United Kingdom gave way to this new superpower.

During the nineteenth century, the financial system followed the gold standard, and the British pound played a pivotal role as the major reserve currency of the world. Then, the United States, Canada, and Australia were ranked among less developed countries. The United Kingdom was the one and only superpower in the world. Under the gold standard, currencies were redeemable into gold. A trade deficit implied that gold flowed out of a country and went to one that had a trade surplus. The balance of exports and imports mandated the flow of gold from one country to another and hence acted as a monetary stabilizer.

The inflation that plagued the world after World War I knocked off the gold standard from 1919 to 1925, as the United Kingdom did not have enough gold reserves to meet convertibility of other foreign currencies. A large amount of gold was shipped to the United States to pay for the massive war debt. This, in turn, caused a severe deflation and a serious drop in commodity prices; in fact, the rest of the world felt the shadow of the depression long before the United States did.

During the early 1920s, Britain's economy weakened and its trade balance suffered from a large deficit. But in 1928, Britain obtained concessions from the New York Federal Reserve Bank to keep interest rates at a level lower than those in the United Kingdom. The purpose of this agreement was to reestablish the gold standard and reinstate the British pound as the reserve currency. At the onset of the worldwide depression, Britain could not fulfill its obligations when gold was demanded for sterling. Finally, on September 21, 1931, the United Kingdom abandoned the gold standard and sterling was floated. This marked the final surrender of Britain as the financial center of the world. The great transition was already well underway.

In 1945, the Bretton Woods conference established the International Monetary Fund as the international lender of last resort and the World Bank as the satisfier of the long-term capital needs of developing countries. The dollar was pegged to gold and became the world reserve currency. By that time, the great transition was complete. The United States became the new political and financial center of the world and emerged as the unchallenged leader of the West. As the British pound resigned its role as the world reserve currency, the dollar assumed that responsibility until 1971, when it was taken off the gold standard and the foreign currency market tasted the swings of the float.

As much as the Great Depression devastated a previous generation, it promised an even greater power to the United States. World political and financial leadership came to North America. The dismal years of the worst economic calamity in U.S. history held a greater challenge and responsibility for the new rising giant.

WHY DID IT HAPPEN?

Economists have been debating the causes of the Great Depression. In all the books and articles that address the subject, there has been no explanation for its severity or for its slow development.

Milton Friedman cited *the massive decline in the money supply induced by the FED as the most important factor behind the depression.* The FED, according to Friedman, maintained a fairly strict monetary policy well after the signs of deterioration were apparent.

John Maynard Keynes, the father of fiscal economic policy, maintained that *the government spent too little too late to stimulate demand.* He explained that monetary policy alone was insufficient to counteract the sharp fall of demand and the loss of consumption that accompanied the collapse. Keynes noted that the depression represented the failure of the free-market system to create enough demand for goods and products. He was in favor of massive government spending to preserve consumption from falling so drastically. He was also in favor of a hybrid system in which government intervenes to halt precipitous cyclical declines in business. *During recessions, the Keynesian approach condones government deficits to vitalize depressed consumption.*

As a matter of fact, Hoover raised taxes during the early stages of the downturn, and Franklin Delano Roosevelt was more concerned with balancing the budget than with the system's illiquidity. When the budget was cut in 1937, the economy tumbled into another severe decline and unemployment rose again.

The experience of the 1930s gave credibility to the Keynesian theory. The economy was unable to overcome the depression without his prescription. It was World War II and its massive government spending that finally put an end to the calamity, only to prove how accurate Keynes' philosophy was. In those days, taxes were very low compared to today's rates; they could not be used successfully to put more money in people's hands in order to stimulate consumption. In later years, when the tax system became more developed, the government learned to lower taxes and run a budget deficit to counteract cyclical declines during recessions. Whether one is for or against government intervention, capitalism was never the same again after the Keynesian revolution—and deservedly so.

John Kenneth Galbraith thought that *the stock market collapse robbed the economy of precious dollars that were badly needed for consumption.* The speculative mania that preceded the crash encouraged businesses to use their excess funds to satisfy stock market margin borrowing. As the brokers' loan rate surged, so did the amount of cash flow that went toward fueling margin activities. Moreover, companies themselves were deeply involved in the equities market, as they reaped higher rates of return on their investments than in their normal business. The total loss that resulted from the crash ballooned to about $74 billion. The melting of wealth accompanied by commodity price deflation devastated consumer spending.

Other economists cited *the speculative overbuilding of residential construction and its collapse in 1928 as major reasons behind the severity of the depression. Household indebtedness reached excessive levels during the 1920s and the system had to go through a process of liquidation of those debts.* Moreover, farmers, who were already in their own depression and represented 20 percent of the employment force, were not in a position to extend beyond their means to stimulate consumption demand. In addition, businesses built up excessive capacity and inventory during the optimistic years, and that led to large shrinkage in the economy.

Some historians thought that *the banking panic had a direct impact on people's net worth.* Over the span of two years, from 1930 to 1932, over 11,000 banks with deposits of more than $7 billion closed their doors. Nine million savings accounts were lost, and about 84,000 businesses went bankrupt due to their inability to withdraw their money from the banks.

The Smoot-Hawley protectionist bill that passed in 1930 was also cited as a major factor behind the depression. It imposed tariffs on imports and was met by retaliation from other foreign countries. The net result was a big shrinkage in international trade that exacerbated the drop in consumption worldwide.

It may have been any of those reasons cited by the Monetarists (such as Friedman), the Keynesians, other economists and historians, or all of them combined. *Complacency, at times, is very costly and painful. It is true that after a full decade of prosperity, one had to be optimistic. People's memory is shortsighted. When things look their best, very few dare to believe that sharp reversals can happen. Mass psychology always swings to extremes and seldom remembers the agony of past disasters.*

It could also have been that these reasons were combined with a long-term cycle that Nicholai Kondratieff, a Russian economist, talked about in the early 1920s. In 1923, his findings, which we will examine later, predicted a depression during the 1930s, citing a long-term cyclical wave that has repeated itself regularly in statistics gathered from several western capitalist economies. Some economists have later explained those observations by the long-term patterns of debt accumulation and debt liquidation.

History tells us that trends do not last forever. Good times are followed by bad times. The roaring twenties culminated in the worst economic debacle in the history of capitalism. After the major downtrend of the 1930s, when people gave up on the future, it was time again for the United States to emerge from the war as a dominant world power. Our journey was, indeed, to hell and back.

❏2

At the Close of the Eighties

Where Are We Today?

"... small events at times have large consequences ... a liquidity crisis in a unit fractional reserve banking system is precisely the kind of event that can trigger—and often has triggered—a chain reaction. And economic collapse often has the character of a cumulative process. Let it go beyond a certain point, and it will tend for a time to gain strength from its own development as its effects spread and return to intensify the process of collapse. Because no great strength would be required to hold the rock that starts a landslide, it does not follow that the landslide will not be of major proportions."

Milton Friedman and Anna Schwartz
Monetary History of the United States 1867–1960

The stock market has long been viewed as the best barometer of the state of business. The financial markets are watched carefully by the highest economic authorities around the world. The Federal Reserve Board (FED) formulates its monetary policy by following developments in 12 leading economic indicators, among which is the stock market. Over the years, the FED has found the latter to be helpful in forecasting the future outlook of business.

Historically, the equities market declined ahead of recessions and advanced well before economic recoveries became apparent. In fact, the stock market predicted the onset of the Great Depression and foresaw the severe contraction of the 1930s. Moreover, it was the first to reflect—ahead of time—the onset of the era of prosperity that followed World War II. The securities market anticipated the turbulence and the runaway inflation of the 1970s. When it comes to predicting the future, financial markets have a track record second to none.

Today's economic environment bears some similarities to those days of the 1920s. Therefore, the pressing questions on many people's minds are: Are we on the verge of another great depression? Can it happen again? What can we do to avert it? What are the similarities and differences between the 1920s and the 1980s? Are there other emerging domestic or international trends that could counterbalance a severe contraction in the economy? What are our options?

The equities crash of 1987 signalled a warning that we cannot afford to ignore. Taking it lightly could be a costly mistake.

REFLECTIONS ON OUR PAST

World War II left behind destroyed cities all over the globe. However, the North American continent was hardly scathed. It was time for the United States to rebuild Europe and help the rest of the world develop. Communism was rising in the East as the United States assumed its responsibility toward its Western allies and defended capitalism. The rise of the multinationals led to an era of great prosperity and economic boom. America became the largest creditor nation and enjoyed two decades of continuous growth. The standard of living surged and political leadership strengthened. This was when America became a world superpower and pioneered the world's most significant technological breakthroughs.

It is probably part of nature's law that good times are followed by bad times. The prosperity of the early 1960s led to social unrest and the early days of declining productivity. The government was concerned about fast economic growth and wanted to slow down the pace of business. Concern about environmental protection and pollution control also gained momentum so, in the late 1960s, corporate America faced heavy taxes and the hefty cost of cleaner air. This combination slowed the economy but the real problems were still a few years away.

In the early 1970s, we were just coming back from the Vietnam War. Inflation was beginning to creep up after years of expansion. In 1971, the Treasury Department, then headed by John Connally, announced the abandonment of the gold standard. From that moment on, gold became the barometer of people's perception of political and currency risks.

In 1973–74, we discovered the mightiest of all cartels, when the Oil-Producing Export Countries (OPEC) suddenly realized that they could corner international markets in the most vital source of energy on earth. The price of oil skyrocketed to $14 per barrel. Long lines of automobiles waited at gas stations, which awakened us to our vulnerability to foreign shocks. The threefold increase in the price of oil affected the production of all U.S. goods and heightened inflation and interest rates.

At the same time, many profound social changes took place. The baby boomers suddenly entered the marketplace and demanded jobs, houses, and a panoply of durable and nondurable goods. The two-paycheck family was also making its mark on society. Women flooded the job market. The rate of divorce was on the rise, and the single household family was becoming acceptable. All these demographic changes were translated into larger consumption demand, which, in turn, exerted further inflationary pressures.

With inflation rising and an abundant supply of labor entering the job market, "stagflation," which occurs when a simultaneous rise in both inflation and unemployment takes place, became a subject of debate. Economists were initially puzzled by this phenomenon.

These demographic changes, as well as external shocks to the economy, combined to lessen the impact of the FED's efforts to balance inflation and unemployment. Interest rates rose to 12 percent and unemployment surged to its highest post-World War II level. From 1973 to 1975, the Western nations fell into the worst recession since the 1930s.

At this point, the service sector grew in leaps and bounds. Administrators and policy makers had to formulate strategies to address all of those new internal and external constraints.

Business suddenly became much more complex, dynamic, and volatile than in the post-World War II era, when growth was achievable in a competition-free world.

Quantum technological innovations and breakthroughs in automation were quickly opening up the marketplace and pushing the economy into unknown territories. Manufacturing in America suffered bruises from Japanese invaders, who kept coming back with all kinds of merchandise. The Japanese invasion of our markets entered a serious phase, beginning with consumer goods such as watches, electronic instruments, cameras, cassette recorders, and televisions. Once successful, the Japanese pressed on to automobiles and computers.

Still counting on the hefty profit margins that the old gas guzzlers were contributing to the bottom line, executives in the U.S. auto industry were taken by surprise. They had failed to recognize the changing character of the marketplace. The Japanese entry into the auto market was well timed because of the energy shortage and changing consumer tastes. Japanese marketers sang about the quality of their cars and were quick to grab a handsome share of the largest car market in the world.

Corporate earnings of U.S. companies came under a serious squeeze and their productivity continued to falter. Exports began to exceed imports, and extravagant spending on luxury items picked up speed. The pain of the trade deficit began to be felt.

In search of a defense mechanism against the cheap labor of Japan, American companies built overseas facilities and resorted to offshore manufacturing. With each cycle of economic contraction, unemployment began to rise to a higher percentage of the working population. Employment in the manufacturing sector began to shrink. This transfer of manufacturing facilities to the Far East helped create new competitors; Korea, Taiwan, Singapore, and Hong Kong began to emerge as new industrial contenders to both Japan and the United States.

The inflationary environment of the 1970s encouraged speculation and compelled people to assume more risk to preserve their net worth. Although the demand for real estate was genuine as the baby boomers formed families, the sky-rocketing price of houses led people to speculate on further price rises. Inflation also led many to speculate on the alluring gold market. All those speculative factors took a severe toll on the economy and helped intensify the inflationary momentum to intolerable levels. Prices rose throughout all sectors of the economy, and corporate profit margins came under severe pressure.

THE DECADE OF SHOCKS

The United States was subjected to many severe economic shocks during the seventies; some had longer-term implications than others. In 1979—as inflation was about to accelerate—the FED hesitated to raise interest rates because they would have crippled capital formation and investment prospects. As a result, inflation in the United States soared to its worst level in the twentieth century.

President Carter was not in an enviable position as he entered the 1980 election. Not only was the country facing severe domestic difficulties, but the international scene appeared equally grim. Iran was causing unrest in the Middle East and threatening to disturb the peace in that strategic part of the world. Russia was pursuing its expansionary goals in Poland and Afghanistan. The Japanese were gaining even more ground and accumulating a huge trade surplus. Europe was suffering from the aftermath of the global recession of 1973–75 and of the hyperinflation caused by the oil shocks.

Understanding the sensitivity of the domestic economic environment, President Carter appointed Paul Volker to the post of chairman of the Federal Reserve Board. Once at the helm of the most influential institution in the Western hemisphere, Volker did not hesitate to hike interest rates to their highest level in the history of modern economics. Interest rates reached the unheard-of peak of 20 percent. The extravagant cost of money finally put a dent in inflation in the early 1980s.

After that, newly elected President Reagan faced a tough job. He had to bring the economy back to health, bring unemployment down, and counteract the expansionary policies of the Soviet Union. Most important, he had to reassure the Western allies of the leadership of the United States.

It took a great deal of communication between Volker and President Reagan to bring the economy back to a path of real growth. Volker acted with prudence as a determined economist who knew exactly the responsibility of his job. He fulfilled his role as a leader who constantly reasserted the FED's commitment to pursue an anti-inflationary policy.

Their hybrid economic policy fought inflation through a stringent monetary policy combined with an expanding fiscal policy. The government borrowed heavily and channelled a good portion of that money into rebuilding the military might of the country. Unfortunately, this liberal fiscal policy created another monster: The budget deficit ballooned and turned us into a debtor nation for the first time since World War II.

In 1981–1982, a serious recession was inevitable. It signalled the beginning of the end of inflation. A tight monetary policy remained in place long after the economic trough was reached, and real interest rates remained at historic highs well after the recession was over.

PAIN IN THE HEART OF MIDDLE AMERICA

During the seventies and throughout the years of zooming inflation, farmers enjoyed massive appreciation of farmland prices and increases in real wealth. In 1972–1973, an extraordinary rise in farm income promised instant prosperity to farmers. Some farmers borrowed heavily to increase those lucrative returns, and there was a rush to leverage. As the values of real estate in the agricultural sector increased, so did the debts of farmers.

Clearly, the continuous advance in prices had toyed with farmers' expectations. The promise of attaching relatively high multiples to farmland earnings eluded most new buyers. And, as inflation abated and incomes fell, land prices plummeted—taking with them the hopes and dreams of long-lasting prosperity in the agricultural sector.

The process of debt liquidation began as early as 1981. Loans were being restructured, and some were liquidated. Rising competition from foreign countries led to an oversupply of agricultural products and exercised downward pressure on food prices. As the decline in food prices continued, debts incurred during the boom years could not be met, and foreclosures became imminent.

Like all other periods of excesses in history, notwithstanding the calamity in the agricultural sector in the early 1920s, borrowers lost their equity and lenders lost a good deal of the funds they had loaned. The impact on the banking system was focused on a group of individual banks making questionable farm loans. In total, about 4,700 banks were involved. Those whose nonperforming loans had exceeded total capital were particularly vulnerable. As many as 200 banks were in this category by early 1986. As the turbulent eighties unfolded, the rate of failure of the agricultural banks rose. Although we had hoped that regulation could bail us out, the farm credit system stood paralyzed in the face of the bust cycle that hit middle America.

The crisis in the agricultural industry may continue into the 1990s. *The process of debt liquidation may persist as long as the disinflation process remains on course.* With it, the jeopardy of more agricultural banks' failures may continue to haunt us for several years to come.

The events that characterized developments in the agricultural sector in the early 1920s and in the 1980s are very similar. They both started with periods of rising inflation. Farmers grew accustomed to rising wealth and a bright future. Their incomes surged and their dreams ran wild with thoughts that the food shortage would persist and that commodity prices and farm incomes would continue to soar for-

ever. Like farmers 60 years ago, they borrowed beyond their means and spent lavishly on machinery and land development. In both cases, difficulties began after commodity prices peaked. The crisis in the agricultural sector of the early twenties continued throughout the thirties, despite the economic recovery. Likewise, although farm debt had peaked in September 1984 and had declined by 20 percent at the end of 1986, the process is still a long way from being over. Today, 60 years later, farmers have to sip from the same cup that their fathers tasted during those years long forgotten.

THE CANDY STORE OF REAL ESTATE

Real estate was the next market to develop speculative excesses, caused by the baby boomers. In the 1970s they reached the age of family formation; it was time to settle down and buy houses of their own. Demand rose and the prices of residential real estate responded. The boom in real estate started on the West Coast, spread from there to Texas, and finally ended up in the Northeast.

Why did it start in the Western states? Probably because of their proximity to the Far East, where Japan and the other progressive newly industrializing countries (NICs) are, and because of the economic boom in that part of the country. It could also have been because of the high percentage of baby boomers in those states.

Texas was the direct beneficiary of the go-go years of the oil price rise. Residing on ample oil reserves and helped by the shocks masterminded by OPEC, it witnessed the best economic boom in its history. There, too, debt became the way to go. The Sunbelt state became the home of rich oil tycoons. The appreciation of both land and residential houses was no less than phenomenal.

Commercial real estate also experienced unparalleled growth. The great service society was accelerating during the seventies, and the demand for office buildings was on the rise. In major cities, a massive number of new prestigious buildings were built to meet that surge in demand. We built more restaurants, travel agencies, and health spas than ever before. We convinced ourselves that those industries would fill the gap left by manufacturing.

The real estate boom was accomplished by speculation. Inflation psychology drove what was a bona fide rise in demand to a full-fledged mania in the housing market. Illusions about striking it rich in real estate became a part of an average investor's expectations. Debt in the household sector rose to unprecedented highs, and savings plummeted.

The huge appreciation in the price of both business and residential real estate properties created an illusive sense of richness. However, every trend has a beginning and an end. Just as it had begun in California, the real estate boom also ended in California, ahead of the other states. Next, the decline travelled to Texas at the wake of the break in oil prices. Rich Texans were humbled by the forces of nature. Bankruptcies mounted and growth stopped. Office buildings were deserted. Suddenly, overcapacity became the new reality in the once lucrative real estate business.

While the rotational depression in real estate was taking its toll on the agricultural sector and oil-rich states, another speculative bubble was on the way. The greatest stock market rise of our generation was announced directly from New York City, the financial capital of the world, which fueled the last speculative gasp in the real estate market.

Once again, the banks extended loans to the masses in what seemed to be the most secure of all markets. After all, who could have foreseen oil prices tumbling from $35 to $15 per barrel? Who would have predicted doom for the Texan millionaires?

When the softness in prices began in California, the troubles of banks with real estate loans also started. Bank America, one of the largest banks in the world, had problems with defaults. In Texas, the sudden melting of oil wealth led to much agony. Several Texas banks were stuck with large questionable loans on their books. In the Northeast, however, real estate experienced healthy growth as rising financial markets brought wealth there. Obviously, that condition became uncertain in the wake of the crash of 1987.

THE HOLLOWING OF THE CORPORATION

The decline in manufacturing that started in the early seventies continued and accelerated throughout that decade and into the eighties. Corporations were challenged by intense competition—both domestic and international—from the Japanese. Falling productivity, rising manufacturing costs, the strict laws on pollution control, the relatively inexperienced labor force dominated by baby boomers, and the resistance of militant unions to compromise or forsake generous benefits contributed to the severe uncompetitiveness that plagued many U.S. industries. Cheap imports and the rush of consumers to buy foreign products, the dumping of goods and raw materials into the U.S. market from all parts of the world, and ineffective, short-term-oriented management strategies led to further declines in companies' fortunes.

The stock market, which failed to adjust securities prices to inflation of the seventies, altered corporate activity on several levels. First, it deprived corporate America of equity financing means. The cash flow that companies badly needed to restructure and regain their competitiveness was denied. The only resource left was borrowing at excessively high interest rates.

The subdued performance of the financial markets led to another problem: Management had to pay more attention to quarterly analysts' reports than to reestablishing their companies' financial health. In sum, short-term economic myopia became the way to survive.

In the early eighties, the dollar became overvalued to the detriment of the basic industrial sector: The strength of the dollar added to the appeal of imports and destroyed our export base. Industry after industry curtailed its domestic manufacturing operations. Many companies relocated their production facilities overseas, where cheap labor could be found, and restructured their businesses to operate as marketing arms to foreign producers.

Thus, the postindustrial economy, which relied on the service sector to provide jobs for the masses, was born. Unfortunately, the service society has never been able to achieve the standard of living that manufacturing had achieved. Over the years, the growth of productivity and income in manufacturing far outstripped that of the service sector. Moreover, the loss of control over resources and capital became a serious issue.

BEYOND THEIR MEANS ... THE CONSUMERS

In a free society, consumers have much to say about the direction of the economy. Their spending or retrenchment determines the demand side of the equation, which in turn drives the supply factors.

According to Surveys of Consumer Finances sponsored by the Board of Governors of the Federal Reserve Board, the U.S. Department of Health and Human Services, and other government agencies, consumer debt has grown substantially to a record high. Installment debt outstanding tripled from $100 billion in 1970 to $337 billion in 1983. It continued to rise at a fast pace to $551.8 billion in 1986. Between 1976 and 1979, it grew at an average compounded annual rate of 15 percent. The economic contractions of 1980 and 1981–1982, accompanied by constraints on the supply of credits, slowed the rate of increase of consumer debt to only 6 percent between 1979 and 1982. However, consumer debt exploded between 1982 and 1987 at an average compounded annual rate of 18 percent.

An important indication of the debt burden's significance is better understood when debt is compared with disposable personal income. In 1987, this ratio reached its highest level since World War II: a hefty 17 percent. Meanwhile, the annual savings rate plummeted to a postwar low of less than 3 percent. According to *Review of the U.S. Economy*, published by Data Resources Inc. on October 1, 1987, consumer expenditures

Figure 2–1. Debt Plague

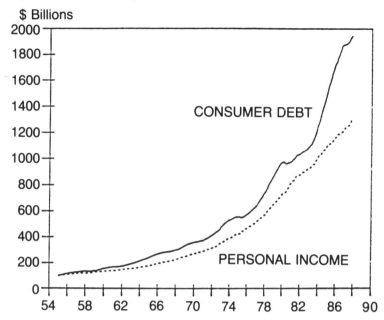

Source: The Commerce Department.

rose 2.2 percent while real disposable income increased by only 0.8 percent.

Consumers substituted credit card debt with mortgage debt in response to the new tax laws. The drop in interest rates and the proliferation of new mortgage instruments led family mortgage debt to grow by 45 percent between 1983 and 1986.

The inflation of the past decade has radically changed consumers' psychology and shifted it toward high-risk territories. Fabulous gains in real estate fueled speculation and encouraged households to expand their leverage.

In the eighties, money became the final frontier. Our fascination with the Midas touch and the magic of easy fortunes reached climactic proportions. The "Lifestyles of the Rich and Famous" became a widely watched television program, just when the stock market was about to greet us with an unpleasant surprise. The front covers of business magazines carried stories about the richest millionaires and successful entrepreneurs. And, as if millionaires were no longer in vogue, some prominent magazines revealed the inner secrets of billionaires.

However, the debt accumulation has now reached an alarming stage that threatens to raise a severe credit risk at the first sign of an economic slowdown. The potential of default is real if unemployment picks up. The result of that loss of income could precipitate a wave of mortgage defaults that could, in turn, severely affect lenders and financial institutions.

The money society of the 1980s and the speculative bubbles that developed in both the housing and financial markets are in jeopardy. The consumption society may finally have to tighten its belt and control its appetite for the luxuries of the past.

IN DEBT WE TRUST

Throughout the 1960s and 1970s, the debt of domestic nonfinancial sectors fluctuated between 136 percent and 138 percent of the gross national product. However, that ratio had risen to 169 percent by the end of 1985 and close to 180 percent by early 1987. Not only has debt risen to alarming proportions in the U.S. economy, but it is deeply entrenched in *all* sectors of the economy, which represents a disturbing change in the country's debt structure. From 1980 to 1985, the total credit market debt of all sectors had expanded from $4.7 trillion to $8.2 trillion.

During the 1981–1982 recession, the government was able to expand its fiscal policy and borrow to stimulate the economy. The government deficit increased dramatically as revenues declined and expenditures grew at a faster pace. A substantial portion of government borrowing went into rebuilding defense. Meanwhile, the tax structure offered liberal depreciation allowances that cut into government revenues. Personal income taxes also decreased and took away another portion of government receipts. The strong economic recov-

Figure 2–2. The Great Credit Society

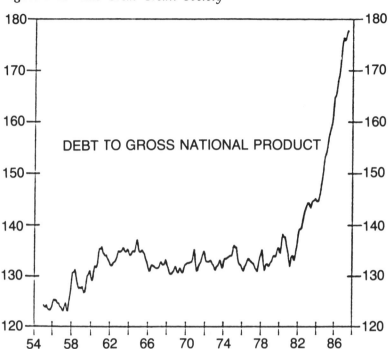

DEBT TO GROSS NATIONAL PRODUCT

Source: The Commerce Department.

ery of 1982–1987 could have enabled the government to reduce the debt that it incurred during the recession. However, the government could not balance the budget, despite cuts in nondefense spending.

On the other hand, economic recovery has always traditionally been associated with an increase in corporate debt. Indeed, corporate debt increased substantially during the first half of the 1980s. That wave of mergers, acquisitions, and leveraged buyouts led to massive equity retirement which was financed through borrowing. In addition, share buy-back programs accelerated in the 1980s. About $200 billion of stocks were retired between 1983 and 1985. In 1986, interest costs represented about 26 percent of corporate cash flow compared with only 19 percent in the 1976–1978 period.

Less developed countries' (LDCs) debt is also astronomical. In the 1970s American banks, awash with OPEC's deposits,
decided that sovereign nations could never go bankrupt. They
recycled their huge money surplus and went on a lending
spree to the LDCs. In 1987, the most troubled 15 debtors among
Third World nations owed about $437 billion to foreign banks,
of which $80 billion was held by American banks. This debt
service is hefty, and the ability of these economies to generate
trade surpluses adequate to pay back those debts is questionable.

*The economy is obviously suffering from a debt plague
that could worsen at the first hint of any slowdown in business activities. Government is carrying a hefty deficit, consumers are overloaded with debt, large amounts of obligations
have replaced equity on corporate balance sheets, and questionable loans to LDCs are huge. Both the scale and pattern of
debt have reached unsustainable proportions.*

Debt liquidation has taken its toll on the economy during
past recessions. The effect was mild in most previous contractions because the debt was much smaller. This time, however,
the burden of debt is at a much higher plateau and could take
some time to be resolved.

WALKING ON THIN ICE ... THE BANKS

In 1985, there were 115 commercial bank failures, the
largest since the Great Depression. In 1986 and 1987, failure
among banks continued unabated. For those who are familiar
with the banking industry, the ailment is not a recent phenomenon; its roots go back in history.

Haunted by the panic of the 1930s, the banking system has
been clobbered with regulations for decades. Thus, when
competition from other sources became excessively intense,
banks were not able to respond successfully. Instead of freeing
our banks from regulations so that they could compete effectively, we held them back and allowed newcomers to gain
market share and prosper.

First, companies such as Ford, Sears Roebuck, and General Motors have had the advantage of being able to extend loans directly to consumers without having to meet reserve requirements. This allowed them to offer financing needs at a lower cost and to compete indirectly with banking institutions. Growth in the size of these nonfinancial organizations allowed them to walk away with a substantial piece of traditional banking.

Next, Japanese financiers shouldered their way into the wide open U.S. market. Awash with cash from their export revenues and free from the FED's reserve requirements, they aggressively proceeded to establish a strong foothold in America. They lent money to states, cities, ailing industries, and failing companies. They financed acquisitions of U.S. companies by Japanese firms and pushed their way through the lucrative financial services on Wall Street. Sumitomo, Namura, and others basically used the aggressive strategy of sacrificing profits for market share. Only a few years ago, U.S. banks dominated the list of the most powerful and richest banks in the world. Today, only Citicorp is still ranked among the top ten; the rest are mostly Japanese.

And last, although the financial services industry grew in the 1970s, explosive growth occurred in the 1980s. The phenomenal rise in equities and fixed income markets around the globe precipitated a corresponding growth in financial services. Investment banking and debt financing grew in leaps and bounds. Mutual funds and new issues skyrocketed, and commissions from regular brokerage business soared.

Again, banks missed out on those heydays of the bonanza in the industry because of their antiquated and cautious financial structure, dating back to the Glass-Steagall Act. Enacted after the banking panic in 1933, it prohibited banks from performing brokerage business and separated commercial and investment banking. The volatility in financial markets led administrators to stand firm, despite the banks' desire to take on the new giants of world banking—the Japanese—as well as the wildest competitors ever seen in the domestic market—giant brokers and insurance companies.

Furthermore, in 1981, Congress removed the lid on interest rates that banks could pay on customer deposits. To compete with money market funds, banks were compelled to pay higher yields on savings and other bank deposits. Higher interest paid out to customers meant more cost and lower profits for the banks. Margins came under squeeze. The proliferation of new innovative banking services—such as NOW accounts, SuperNOW accounts, and electronic fund transfer—added to the banks' cost of doing business.

The debt plague in the domestic and international economies compounds further the banks' troubles. The government, corporations, and consumers are highly leveraged and real estate is overextended. However, business loans, which used to represent a respectable portion of banks' portfolios, decreased in number. In the 1980s, major companies with good credit ratings were able to sell commercial papers directly to big investors through public offerings. The spread between the interest charged on business loans and the cost of funds to banks narrowed to the point where banks became unmotivated to extend such loans unless they could sell them quickly to foreign banks and other financial institutions. The decline in blue-chip corporate lending hurt the profits of large banks. Furthermore, the quality risk of their loan portfolios suffered as blue-chip corporate lending was replaced by higher-risk customers who could be charged higher rates.

International lending looked even more tenuous. LDCs suddenly came to light as potential defaults. Sovereign countries, we were told, never go bankrupt—but they can surely default. As the world economic pie shrunk, so did the export revenues of Third World countries. In total, with some $80 billion at risk, banks are struggling to defuse the bomb. In a bold move, Citicorp led major U.S. banks in adding some $3 billion to its reserves against LDC loans. The problem is far from over, especially now that the world economic outlook suggests further sluggishness into the 1990s.

PROTECTIONISM IS BACK

In the 1980s, the ghost of protectionism and trade wars between nations reappeared. With a stagnant global economy and faltering commodity prices, nations adopted trade policies that imposed nontariff barriers. Third World countries were particularly hard hit, since raw materials constitute the bulk of their export revenues. The worldwide decline in commodity prices impacted their balance of payments. In order to prevent a total collapse and to avert a risk of default on their huge loans, we had to open our markets and act as the economic locomotive of a faltering world economy.

Meanwhile, the Japanese were unrelentingly dumping their products on our domestic market. Their market share expanded and their trade surplus ballooned. While we kept our markets open for free trade, Japan denied American companies the opportunity to compete in its market. Not only did Japanese companies invade our markets, but they used the same tactics in other corners of the globe. While several Western nations refrained from trading with South Africa, Japan aggressively pursued its dominance in that country and increased its share of trade. Japan is now South Africa's largest trading partner. Although Japan was asked to exercise voluntary restraints, relief was temporary. Wave after wave of unfair attacks on markets around the world was launched.

Japan is not the only nation that did not abide by the rules of free trade. Several countries around the world adopted policies to restrict importation of goods and asked other nations to respect the General Agreement on Tariffs and Trade. They had little faith in the benefits of equitable trade and perceived free trade as a threat to their domestic industries.

Meanwhile, our trade deficit reached alarming proportions and the crisis became unsustainable. U.S. corporate profits declined and margins were squeezed. In search for an answer, American companies sought cheap labor and overseas manufacturing. What used to be the exception evolved into a full-fledged exodus of manufacturing. This, in turn, led to further declines in our competitive position in manufacturing and threatened the transfer of our know-how and technology to other countries. The more our trade deficit grew, the more Washington came under fire to do something about the Japanese. Senators and Congressmen alike were demanding: Open up your market or we will close ours. Token progress was achieved and the crisis was defused with warm words of friendship.

THE SHARP HORNS OF THE BULL

During the summer of 1982, the business environment was not promising and the country was in a recession. The government budget deficit was cause for alarm, and unemployment was on the rise. There were prophecies of gloom and doom everywhere. We were told that we should prepare ourselves for hard times ahead. We were greeted with books that tried to convince us that we should hoard food and weapons to defend ourselves against the oncoming chaos.

Interest rates were still close to their highs for this century and the stock market was struggling at around 800. Then, volume was considered active when it exceeded 40 million shares. The runaway inflation of the seventies left behind an investment community that was skeptical of the outlook for equities. Thus, for an entire decade, the market was subdued and the Dow Jones Industrial Average stumbled and had difficulty surpassing 1050.

Yet on August 12, 1982, the bull market of the 1980s began. A stampede pulled the market from below 800, on very high volume, to the low 900s. Amid skepticism and confusion, it proceeded to 1050. All it took was three months to push the market to a level that, in the past, used to take a couple of years to reach.

Although the budget deficit and interest rates remained high and went even higher, the bull market continued on course. The economy rebounded in late 1982 and a solid business recovery started. Meanwhile, the stock market expanded to new territories. By the end of 1983, the Dow Jones had advanced to 1300. Then, after undergoing a healthy consolidation, the market resumed its advance in August 1984.

For the next three years, the bull market was no less than sensational, even though the Japanese were rising to prominence in international trade. However, consumer debt rose to its highest level in the past three decades, the budget deficit ballooned, corporate debt exploded in the wake of the takeover mania, and the economy meandered sluggishly. Every time the advance hesitated, the voice of the bears predicted doom and gloom. Yet the market ignored all these prophecies and resumed its advance with a vengeance—on a steep upward path.

From August 1984 to August 1987, the Dow Jones Industrial Average advanced from around 1100 to an all-time high of 2746.65—almost a 270 percent appreciation in three years. During the summer of 1987, the rise was particularly breathtaking. Money became the ultimate frontier, gains were abundant, and the market seemed to be gathering strength. At that point, analysts and investors alike were fully convinced that the market was heading higher. Apparently, greed blinded them to the alarming fundamentals. And little did the world know what the future held in store.

SPECULATION IN THE EIGHTIES

During the bull market of 1982 to 1987, equities advanced substantially. But despite the phenomenal rise in stock prices, adjusted for inflation, equities were not out of line relative to their underlying value. In fact, they were undervalued. On the other hand, the acquisition mania may have been fueled by the tremendous appreciation of corporate real estate holdings that was not reflected in the price of the stock or the high liquidity that large investors had.

The investment community was thrilled with the takeover game, yet they forgot that it reached excesses far beyond the fair valuation of corporate assets. Instead of concentrating on what they do best, corporate management became more concerned with weathering hostile takeovers. They bought back their own shares and formulated new strategies to discourage aggressors. What became known as the "poison pill" automatically gave shareholders a large number of shares with which to fend off unfriendly acquisitions. All in all, corporate America assumed additional debt to defend itself.

Despite these measures, takeovers continued unabated on Wall Street in the eighties. No company—small or large— could escape it. The big companies had giant suitors after them. RCA was acquired by General Electric and General Foods by Philip Morris. Adding to this were corporate raiders who stalked Wall Street looking for prey. They were not genuinely interested in acquiring other companies, but were in it for the large sums of money they stood to gain from the process. Once a raider acquired a decent portion of a targeted company's stock, an announcement of the acquisition was made public. When the price of the security advanced, the would-be acquirer sold out—at which point the price plummeted. Similarly, in the 1920s there were pools of operators who ran campaigns in stocks to push their prices artificially higher.

Some investors realized large gains from these deals that characterized the decade. They did not have to be smart or aggressive; all they had to do was be shareholders of one of those companies that were targeted for those activities. Some of those investors stayed too long and saw their gains evaporate after the acquisition was aborted. A few speculators got hurt because they bought on the announcement, after the stock had already moved. As there were instances in which the initial price offered was followed by a higher one, some were encouraged to buy on the initial announcement, hoping for a higher bid. It also made those who were already holding stock wait for the next bid. In some cases investors saw their profits disappear, and those who bought after the initial advance often assumed a loss.

Options, futures, and options on futures added further volatility to the market of the eighties. They allured people to assume risk in pursuit of illusory profits and encouraged short-term speculation rather than investment in the future of America. They gave rise to a whole new breed of speculators, who became interested in intra-day activities and hourly fluctuations. Options on baskets of stocks were created and others on indexes were formulated. And computer programs greeted us every third week of the month with violent and unexplained market reactions.

Daily fluctuations grew more and more influenced by options activities. Wall Street was tagged the casino society. Investors were required to guess rather than invest—and the guessing game finally had to come to an end.

FROM WALL STREET TO LASALLE STREET ... THE TERROR SPREADS

On Wall Street sits the venerable New York Stock Exchange, where billions of dollars exchange hands every day. On LaSalle Street sits the Chicago Board of Trade, where hundreds of millions of dollars of option contracts are traded daily. On October 19, 1987, both streets witnessed a historic event: the worst single day decline in the history of the stock market. On that one day, the Dow Jones Industrial Average dropped a stunning 508 points, or 23 percent of its value. The volume was 604 million shares—more than the entire number of shares traded during 1957.

This one-day, big-bear market devastated the wealth of millions of investors and shattered the faith of the masses in a safe world. We almost went over the brink. The intensity of the collapse in the value of corporate securities was scary. Those agonizing hours of the melting of wealth became etched into the minds of investors around the globe exactly as Black Tuesday had in 1929.

On Sunday night, October 18, 1987, markets around the world opened downward. New Zealand led the way, followed by Australia, Japan, and the United Kingdom. In New York, the massive liquidation was on course the following day. Major institutions rushed to the sell side. Giant mutual funds sold millions of shares to meet redemption. At 10:30 A.M., the Dow was already down 104 points. Half an hour later, the market was down 208 points. All the fail-safe systems that were built in suddenly disappeared. The selling of index futures created a vacuum that removed all support from securities prices. Neither earnings, intrinsic value, nor fancy blue-chip names held back the avalanche.

In a moment of truth, there were no value investors left; there were simply no buyers, and the stock market showed its power to wipe out wealth. General Motors lost 16 points to close at $50, Exxon dropped 8.5 points to close at $35, Manufacturers Hanover plummeted 9.5 points to close at $27, United States Steel declined 13 points to $21, Walt Disney slipped 19 points, GTE was down by almost 10, Digital Equipment lost 42, and Procter & Gamble tumbled a hefty 23 points. The blood list was long. No stock escaped the knockout punch. The Rolls-Royces of corporate America could not be separated from the small and fragile stocks.

The shock echoed throughout the world. There was no other subject more important than that historic event, including Middle East mishaps, Persian Gulf wars, hyperinflation in Argentina, and defaults of LDCs. If judged by historic standards, the meaning of that decline brought alive the ultimate threat of the replay of the thirties. Panicky voices shouted at Washington to balance the deficit. Others took their fury out on computerized trading and portfolio insurance.

On October 20, 1987, the FED announced that it would stand behind the banks. The FED's message was: Lend brokers money and worry about it later. Many stocks suspended trading. At that stage, the system was unable to endure another wave of selling. The crisis had reached alarming proportions that threatened the total collapse of Western civilization. Corporations came in large numbers to support their own stocks. For a brief moment, the wounded specialists seemed unable to maintain liquidity and support prices. The fragility of the system was only too clear to the naked eye. The market was neither fair nor orderly and the party was over. Dreams of the elusive Dow 3200, which had previously seemed a sensible goal, soon evaporated. These dreams were replaced with concerns about the economy and the future course of business. Tighten your belt, brother, a recession is around the corner, some experts said.

No one can tell if the crash of 1987 is a believable prophecy of doom. Even after the 1929 collapse, the market rebounded for a while. The real danger was crystallized over the course of many years. An election year in 1988 could add more confusion to what the real stock market message may have been. It may be an aberration, but a bear market is also credible. Yet the intensity of the decline can only be understood over the course of the coming years.

❏ 3

A Voice from the Plains of Siberia

The Kondratieff Prophecy

"Since we are the prisoners of what we know, often we are unable even to imagine what we don't know. ... Man, given the proper initiative and freedom to act, has repeatedly found alternatives to ambiguity and doom."

Walter B. Wriston
Retired chief executive of Citicorp

Cycles in the history of mankind have been recognized since time immemorial. The recurrence of fluctuation in agriculture and in industrial production has been acknowledged and studied over the years. The Bible tells of a time in ancient history that witnessed a period of great prosperity, which was followed by a severe economic slowdown. The story goes that the Pharaoh had a dream, which he asked Joseph to interpret. Recognizing the time element and the subtleties of the cycle theory, Joseph was able to decipher the Pharaoh's dream of seven years of prosperity followed by seven years of famine. In fact, the theory of prosperity followed by depression is well entrenched in the history of the free enterprise system.

In 1926, a Russian economist, Nicholai Dimitrievich Kondratieff, revealed the results of a study he had conducted on commodity price behavior over a long span of time. His research indicated that a long-term cycle of 50- to 60–years' duration existed in capitalist economies. As a result, he concluded that a depression was possible in the 1930s. When his papers were published, very few Western economists heeded them. But once the devastating depression hit, his observations were elaborately reexamined.

Although the long-term cycle was neither proven to be valid nor refuted, we would like to review the tenets of that theory, especially in light of the many similarities between the twenties and the eighties. During both periods, the agriculture sector suffered a depression, there was rampant real estate speculation, there was a great bull market, and then the stock market crashed.

Since the Great Depression, we have designed an elaborate safety net to prevent the dismal episode from recurring. Still, we cannot afford to let optimism override prudence. We should heed the stock market's warnings well and examine carefully all possibilities. Over the years, the stock market has proven to be a valuable barometer of future economic conditions. In the past, it has forecasted economic recoveries, as well as recessions, long before they became apparent in statistics. In today's world of mammoth institutions, a major failure could quickly spread into other sectors of the economy and lead to similar, unpleasant consequences.

VISION BEYOND BELIEF

Nicholai Dimitrievich Kondratieff was born in Russia in 1892. At the age of 25, he served as deputy minister of food in Alexander Kerensky's government. By 1920, he had founded and directed the Moscow Business Research Institute. Between 1922 and 1925, he wrote several papers that investigated the long-term cycle that appeared to recur in capitalist economies every 50–60 years. His essays resulted from the study of several European economies. They revealed the recurrence of super-long-term cycles in commodity prices, interest rates, inflation, and several other economic aggregates.

Kondratieff postulates that capitalist economies endure cycles of a long-term nature. His theory was rejected by socialists because it defied Marx's prediction of a total demise of the West. Contrary to communist beliefs, Kondratieff concluded that *capitalist economies go through those long cycles to rectify the cumulative imbalances that develop during phases of expansion. He believed that this was a process of rejuvenation that Western economies experienced during the course of their development.*

Kondratieff himself did not mean his study to be a theory but rather an observation of economic behavior over a long span of time. Then, the science of gathering information and data was at best hazy and fragmented. No one followed up on his statistics because it took too long to gather and verify such data. Because of his many political enemies, Kondratieff was accused of treason by the Communist party. He was then condemned to a prison in Siberia, where he died without ever knowing whether his observations were valid. His voice, however, reached the highest corners of academia in the West and is still echoing across the mountains to remind us of the tidal wave.

THE REJUVENATION OF CAPITALISM

Kondratieff's observations anticipated the Great Depression almost five years before it happened. When his prophecy came true, Western economists reexamined his findings.

A split opinion was in order. Paul Samuelson, the dean of modern economics of our time, rejected Kondratieff's postulates as Russian rhetoric and a statistical absurdity. Meanwhile, Joseph Schumpeter, under whom Samuelson had studied economics at Harvard in the 1930s, acknowledged the possibility that such a long-term cycle may exist. Schumpeter himself was a savvy student of cycles and wrote two volumes entitled *Business Cycles* in 1939. In fact, Schumpeter explained the severity of the 1930s depression as a result of the culmination of several business cycles that occurred simultaneously.

The Kondratieff wave (K-wave) had other strong supporters among university professors and academicians. Walt Whitman Rostow, former advisor to Presidents Kennedy and Johnson and professor of economics at the University of Texas, popularized the theory in his book *The World Economy*. Jay Forrester, a professor at MIT, also confirmed the validity of Kondratieff's supercycle and tried to explain it in terms of long cycles in both consumer goods and capital goods. In several of his speeches, Nobel Prize winner and Princeton University economist Sir Arthur Lewis supported the existence of long-term cycles of prosperity and contraction in Western economies.

The cyclical nature of business is well accepted by prominent economists and astute traders. There is an intuitive appeal to the postulates of the K-wave and its forecasting potential. Western economies *are* cyclical in nature. From an even broader perspective, one should accept the ideology of cycles and trends in the economy as well as in politics, finance, and social movements. The interrelationships of these cycles and their evolution accentuate or negate their outcome. In fact, fads and temporary mass psychology could, at times, impact those cycles and make them even more pronounced.

The process of contraction and expansion of the supply/demand balance is constantly fluctuating around an equilibrium path of growth. Throughout history, it has been noted that prolonged periods of prosperity are followed by an unavoidable—at times even painful—retrenchment. Those years of prosperity encourage complacency and open the door for speculation and disequilibrium.

Cycles of severe inflation prompt administrators to adhere to stringent economic policies until inflation subsides. For a while, however, the psychology of both the public and the administrators continues to focus on the problem of inflation. At such junctures, the failure to recognize that the crisis has been resolved leads to further action that exacerbates the trend in the opposite direction. Eventually, deflation is recognized as the new issue to address. In the interim, violent economic swings materialize and, if not handled with care, could lead to serious repercussions.

The long wave is thought by some economists to be a process of redistribution of wealth. During several decades of business growth, inefficiency and excesses build within the system. Then debt accumulates to such a level that it makes the system vulnerable to a shakeout. A phase of debt liquidation that takes a few years to complete ensues. Once this process takes its toll on the economy, the system is debt light again and reinvestment accelerates. The free enterprise system shrugs off the inefficiencies that develop during the years of economic expansion and the excesses of speculation in financial markets. It is a process through which capitalism rejuvenates and positions itself for future growth. The logic behind this explanation of long-term cycle phenomena is sound. Cycles of long duration such as the one that Kondratieff uncovered, which deal with major corrective and structural processes, should be considered in formulating economic policies.

The purpose of this chapter is to examine the tenets of the Kondratieff wave within the context of the business environment at the close of the eighties. In our opinion, the theory is at best incomplete and is based on highly fragmented statistics, the reliability of which is uncertain. We are incorporating it into our discussion for illustrative purposes of various possibilities. Integrating these possibilities into our investigation could help us to better understand the current economic environment and to sharpen our assessment of choices and solutions.

Kondratieff's prophecy should not be considered a *fait accompli*. Indeed, it is hard to be fatalistic in today's day and age, when we have reached the stage where our civilization aspires toward establishing permanent stations in space. It is erroneous to accept that our world is governed by mysterious waves against which we are totally helpless. Kondratieff's findings defy the ability of Western civilization to control its destiny. It undermines the capacity of the free enterprise to create opportunities for future generations. It presumes our inability to exercise our options and to spring forward toward higher pedestals of accomplishments.

Instead of yielding to Kondratieff's deterministic predictions, we should react to its gloomy prophecy with the best of economic strategies. It is only natural that our advanced world of intellectual sophistication and know-how refuses to be governed by the so-called "laws of nature." It is our collective reaction to economic adversities that shapes our destiny and dampens their consequences on our lives. The legacy of a constantly changing world and the evolution of new institutional structures have taken the human race to ever higher standards of progress.

Because Kondratieff's work was accomplished before the Great Depression of the 1930s, many students of economics accepted his theory as a probability that only the future may prove valid. As much as his theories seem remote, we have several sectors of the economy that have been undergoing a severe adjustment since the early eighties. Some have already fallen into a painful slowdown that approximates the dimensions of the worst recessions of the past, including the thirties. We are plagued with debt at the corporate, government, consumer, and international fronts. Moreover, we are witnessing a severe decline of competitiveness in industry and manufacturing. Given the delicate stage we are at in our history, there should be no time for complacency. Whether we credit Kondratieff or otherwise, the message is that history testifies to the recurrence of tragedies when mankind does not take the precautions necessary to prevent them.

THE KILLER WAVE

Our discussion of the K-wave is based on an essay entitled "Long Economic Cycles" that was written by Kondratieff himself. It was published in the journal *Voprosy Konyunktury (Problems of Economic Conditions)*, Volume I, No. 1,

1925. This paper was translated in its entirety in a book entitled *The Long Wave Cycle* by Guy Daniels, introduced by Julian M. Snyder, and published by Richardson & Snyder in 1984.

Although Kondratieff himself admitted that long-term cycles are very difficult to study or conceptualize, he described the long wave as comprising three phases: the upswing, the crisis, and the downswing. The major focus of his research was commodity prices. He examined data on a series of prices from France dating back to 1850. He also compared patterns of his findings on prices from England, Germany, and the United States as far back as 1780.

Besides commodity prices, Kondratieff studied cyclical patterns in the following economic aggregates:

❑ Interest rates, based on data on the discount rate and interest-bearing securities in both France and England.

❑ Nominal wages, based on the weekly wages of workers in the cotton industry in England.

❑ Foreign trade turnover, based on total exports and imports from England and France.

❑ The production and consumption of coal, pig iron, and lead in France, England, Germany, and the United States.

❑ The portfolio of the Banque de France and deposits in French savings accounts.

Using Kondratieff's own words, "On the basis of available data, it *may* be *assumed* that the existence of a long economic condition is very *probable*." Before we proceed with our discussion, let us turn to the words "may," "assumed," and "probable" in his statement. It appears that Kondratieff did not wholeheartedly stand behind his conviction. We emphasize these words to point out that we are not dealing with a well-founded theory. Rather, we are merely entertaining the possibilities of some of Kondratieff's observations.

THE KONDRATIEFF PROPHECY

As a result of his statistical analysis, Kondratieff made the following observations:

1. *There exists a long wave cycle in capitalist economies with a duration of 48–55 years.* The time series studied indicated troughs around 1790, 1845, and 1895. Peaks materialized roughly around 1815, 1870, and 1920. *The beginning of the down wave,* according to the K-wave model, *coincides with an important peak in commodity prices.* Although Kondratieff analyzed data only through 1925, the Great Depression of the 1930s was considered to be the trough of a wave peaking in 1920. Moreover, based on his observations, a peak in business activities that coincided with a peak in commodity prices materialized in 1980.

2. *The commodity price rise and hyperinflation that are heightened around major economic peaks are induced by wars or changes in the population that lead to an increased demand for goods.* As supply and production lag, the sudden rise in demand and the pressure on prices mount. Interest rates rise to extreme levels, which seem to put a dent in the trend of inflation.

3. Following the major turning point and at the onset of the downswing, a severe recession sets in. Shortly thereafter, *a full-fledged depression develops in the agricultural sector.* Although the economy slowly begins to recover from that severe recession, it never regains the momentum it had prior to the peak in commodity prices and farmland prices continue to move downward. The depression in agriculture worsens. The next few years following the peak of a K-wave are tagged *a plateau dominated by slow growth and a lackluster economy. Deflation follows the years of inflation after that major turning point in the cycle. The downside pressure of deflation eventually brings about a wave of debt liquidation, accompanied by a severe business slowdown or depression.* During those years of the downswing, the economic slide is interrupted by short

spurts of recovery that are followed by reacceleration of the downside pressure. The intensity of the decline at the end of the wave is precipitous and leads to a total wash-out.

4. Around the peak of the long wave and during the early phases of the downswing, *great technological discoveries and major breakthroughs in new methods of production are discovered.* Those new techniques, however, are not fully utilized by the economy until the early stages of the next upswing.

5. After the downswing takes its toll on the system and a major trough is at hand, the ensuing upswing starts slowly and sporadically. Prices gradually begin to recover at a slow rate; capital investment and consumption start to pick up. As the upswing progresses, business accelerates and continues to expand, interrupted by only brief intermediate adjustments. Those corrections in the major trend are recognized as mild recessions that are a part of the business cycle.

In order for us to assess where we stand in the eighties, we should test these findings with the actual business environment. Some recent economic developments may fit those observations made by Kondratieff. Although they may have been a coincidence, they should still be acknowledged. Despite the safety net that we have built over the years, some business sectors have suffered a great deal in the early eighties. Given the historic stock market decline in 1987, we should ask ourselves if it may be giving us a message that is stronger than we had thought.

SIGNS OF THE TIMES

A review of the business environments of the 1920s and the 1980s leads us to the following observations:

1. World War I triggered a substantial rise in commodity prices and farmlands which was met by a corresponding

advance in interest rates in the late 1910s. Sixty years later, the sudden demand for a variety of goods and products by baby boomers, oil price shocks, costly pollution control measures, the invasion of our markets by the Japanese, and volatile and destabilizing monetary policies led to an environment of severe inflation. Interest rates reached an extreme level—at around 20 percent—in the early 1980s. Inflation subsided and the results were greeted satisfactorily by financial markets.

2. *The abatement of inflationary pressures in the early 1920s was followed by a depression in agriculture,* which led to the bankruptcy of many farmers and several agricultural banks. *In the early 1980s, inflation declined* and the agricultural sector followed the same pattern it had in the early 1920s: *a depression developed there,* which has claimed the fortunes of farmers and lenders alike.

3. The economy went into a severe recession after interest rates skyrocketed in the early 1920s. *The 1921–1922 recession was the initial adjustment to the rising prices that fol-*lowed World War I. *Sixty years later, we endured the 1981–1982 severe recession, which followed the fast rise in interest rates* that materialized in 1980.

4. *Speculation in real estate began in the early 1920s and reached its peak around 1926.* The same thing happened 60 years later. *In the 1980s, real estate became an investor's haven; prices were expected to go up forever.* Speculation started in California in the late 1970s and boomed in Long Island, New York in 1985.

5. *During the 1920s, household debt reached intolerable levels.* It was eventually stopped by massive liquidation and severe unemployment. For many families, the pressure lasted for a decade. In the 1980s, *the ratio of debt to personal income has reached an unsustainable level—*above 17 percent. Also, the savings rate is at its lowest point since World War II.

6. *The stock market's historic advance of the 1920s led to overspeculation* and ended abruptly with the crash of 1929,

which correctly predicted the onset of the Great Depression. Sixty years later, the stock market started its historic rise from 1982 to 1987 and also ended abruptly with the crash of 1987. The magnitude of both declines far outstrips all others in the twentieth century.

7. *In the early 1920s, banks—especially in the agricultural lending business—failed.* In the 1980s, the depression in agriculture and faltering real estate claimed many banks that were extended in those sectors. Large international banks are also haunted by the shadow of less developed countries' (LDCs) default. They have also overextended themselves with takeovers, megadollar deals, and junk bonds on Wall Street—the result of which is still not clear.

Besides these similarities, the 1980s have even further economic problems. There is an eroding competitiveness of our manufacturing base, as many industries have been severely dislocated by foreign invaders, led by the Japanese. A shift has been quietly taking place from an industry-based economy to a service-oriented one. Capacity utilization has been excessive, productivity has been low, and the economy of the mid-1980s has been, at best, sluggish.

A TEST OF OUR RESOLVE

Today, 60 years after Kondratieff announced his observations yet could not explain their cause, we are faced with the same dilemma. There are some similarities in business developments in the twenties and the eighties. The process that leads to painful, long-term economic adjustments appears to evolve in the same order of events. While we should look upon our world's future with optimism, we have to deal with the facts; we have to devise solutions to ensure that the agonizing thirties are not repeated again, despite the many warning signs.

The process of long-term deterioration always starts with a period of skyrocketing inflation that is unequivocally accompanied by substantial appreciation in farm wealth. Interest rates rise in an attempt to control inflation from getting out of hand. Inflation subsides and commodity prices tumble. Problems in the agricultural sector develop. A serious contraction takes its toll on farmers, leading to massive liquidation and disastrous consequences for both borrowers and lenders.

The psychology of inflation, which becomes deeply ingrained into people's future expectations, leads to speculation in the housing market and real assets. Like the agricultural speculation bubble that precedes it, overspeculation in real estate raises prices up to exorbitant levels. During that process, consumers get more and more deeply into debt. For a while, prices of real estate keep promising an even brighter outlook. Banks and savings and loans, which earlier fell into the trap of agricultural lending, now commit themselves to mortgage debts that later prove to be unsound.

With people's complacency and illusory sense of richness, the stage is now set for financial assets to have their turn. The stock market stampedes and continues to move to unheard-of levels for several years until no one is bearish. At that stage, people think that things are different and that they know better. This marks the third—and last—bubble in the series of developments before the final adjustment, when the process of debt liquidation begins. The stock market plummets, warning that the adjustment has started.

During this process, banks continue to extend loans to individuals and corporations. Later, as the correction begins, many of those borrowers become big liabilities when they default on loans. In the 1920s, the banks fueled the stock market speculation. In the 1980s, the banks financed a takeover mania.

The money society of the eighties has been extensively written about in the media. Stories of the rich and famous and their lifestyles have become the hottest subject on television. Front-page feature articles are in a constant race to report who has what and who is richer than whom. This phony sense of

prosperity has blinded many among us to important issues
that have to be addressed.

Finally, there seems to be a sequential pattern that develops over several decades to bring about a severe corrective phase in business. Those adjustments rectify the excesses that have built up during the prior decades of growth. At the close of the eighties, this process appears to have started. There are quite a few issues that our nation has to consider as we enter the 1990s. Those consolidations that occur in our economy are not necessarily evil. We should accept them as part of the rejuvenation process that the business environment has to go through in order to grow again. We should consider them to be a means whereby the free enterprise system rids itself of cumulative inefficiencies. It is a test of our resolve and a challenge to our strength as a nation to prepare ourselves for a brighter future.

The debt accumulated through borrowing on credit cards, margins, and second mortgages has to be liquidated at some point for the system to rejuvenate itself. It is this liquidation process that is painful and tiring. But our options are many. We should seize the opportunities presented to us to emerge as a greater nation. Given the inner talent and know-how that we have amassed over years of progress, we can conquer all adversities. The solution to our declining standard of living should emanate from a deep understanding of today's business environment. We did it before and we shall do it again now.

THE TASK AHEAD OF AMERICA

By now, we have examined the evolution of the events that led to the Great Depression. We have also reviewed the state of business in the eighties. There are some similarities that cannot be ignored. The facts go beyond complacency and the soothing and reassuring words of politicians. They should command the total attention of the people, corporations, and our administrators. We should therefore move decisively to rebuild our competitiveness. We should team up as a nation to prevent Kondratieff's prophecy from coming true and to take on the challenge of our generation.

The farmers of the eighties are encountering the same fate as their ancestors of the twenties. The equities crash of 1987 was not an aberration that could be tackled as a temporary adjustment. The speculative real estate bubble, reminiscent of the twenties, is not a fluke that can be ignored. Added to this, the alarming debt in the eighties mirrors that of the twenties.

Back in the twenties, there was no reference point with which to compare the catastrophe. Today, after reaching the highest standard of living ever achieved in the history of mankind, we cannot afford to close our eyes, bury our heads in the sand, and say all will be all right. Instead, we have to recognize the challenges that we face and react to resolve the issues at hand.

The next few years are going to add an important chapter to our history as a great nation. The twenties witnessed a transition from an agrarian society to an industrial one, and the eighties marked the beginning of our evolution from an industrial to a postindustrial society. The hybrid society ahead of us is a combination of industry and service; it should accommodate manufacturing and seek a steeper growth path in the service sector. We have, as a nation, accepted the challenge of growth throughout our long history as leaders of the free world. And now, the pressure is on us to do the best we can to preserve our standard of living and lead the world to greener frontiers.

Today's modern business know-how presents us with a large menu of preventive measures from which to choose. The modern entrepreneur is armed with sophisticated tools to implement growth strategies. In search of solutions, we should also rethink our past and examine our options to reshape America. Despite the similarities between the twenties and the eighties, we can also cite many differences, which are addressed in detail in later chapters. It is more important to understand the critical challenges we are faced with at this point. Our world has changed from a demographic, sociological, technological, and psychological standpoint. We live in a globally interdependent economy. We are no longer competing with ourselves as we used to, and the political environment has radically changed; the world has several superpowers that can change the course of history. Some of the greater challenges that we face are outlined below.

We cannot live today in isolation from the events that surround us as a nation. Since we are the protectors of democracy, the globalization of the world economy presents us with a challenge. While reestablishing our industrial superiority in the global context, we should help other nations to face the century to come with dignity. Having learned from our past experience, we should strive to prevent protectionism from becoming epidemic. A trade war among nations could have a devastating effect in an environment of slow growth.

The rise of Japan Inc. is another challenge to our existence as an industrial superpower. It has been fascinating to watch that nation rise from the ashes of its defeat in World War II to become a legend in its own right. The Japanese have earned their status as supermanufacturers who have sold their products in every corner of the world. They have challenged the mighty industrial countries in their own markets and gained respect. An unstoppable Japan has awakened the world to new norms of success. Determination and hard work can still do wonders, and Japan is an example of that accomplishment. Facing up to the Japanese challenge should be among our top priorities in the coming years.

Reasserting our overall manufacturing superiority in the world market should be another of our major targets in the future. Revitalization of our manufacturing sector is critical in order to command control over our resources. The unrealistic dream of the great service society of the future cannot compensate for the absence of manufacturing. As a nation, we should gear up our resources and compete in the global economy. We should devise ways to improve our productivity, and we should bring our manufacturing facilities back home to America.

We are fortunate that technology can now resolve the shortages that other generations have suffered. It holds the promise of new avenues of wealth and growth. It creates prosperity and generates a whole new spectrum of opportunity. There is quite a big difference between today's technology and the technology of the twenties. Earlier in this century, technology opened new horizons for people. The commercial growth of the automobile industry led to a boom in many existing sectors, such as steel and basic materials. Highways and roads were paved. Cities were redesigned to make room for increased traffic. Gasoline stations were built and pipelines were extended. None of the above expansion required more than minimal training for new entrants into the job market. However, today's technology, despite its great promise, requires a highly skilled labor force. To attain this goal, we have to overhaul our training and educational base. Technology offers good potential for our future outlook, but it also compels us to plan for a more sophisticated world.

There is no crystal ball that can guide us through the course of future events. As Volker walked on thin ice—facing runaway inflation—Alan Greenspan should lead us through the debt liquidation process. Administrators should focus on reliquification of the financial markets to support a soft landing of the economy.

Kondratieff's prophecy may just be an observation that applies to the past. It does not have to haunt our perception of the future. The prophecy suggests that our life on earth is governed by powers outside our control. It omits mention of human ingenuity and its power to conquer adversities and overcome hardships. The roaring twenties are long gone, but it pays for us to reexamine our past. Human errors could happen again, and their cumulative effects could make a history that no one would like to live through. Conscious action to rectify the excesses that were built over the years could spare us surprises.

The Great Depression of the thirties was caused mainly by deflation. Today, we are much smarter, more informed, and more capable of controlling our destiny—or at least that is what we think. History is written by what we collectively do.

The economy and the world could live with inflation, but the cost of deflation is too high and should be ruled out. We do not claim that this book can map out an infallible strategy to deal with our future challenges. We rather strive to faithfully present the state of affairs as they exist today, as well as a menu of options from which to choose. Awareness of where we came from and where we stand is an important step toward understanding the extent of the challenge that we are facing. For the balance of this book, we study today's business environment. Along the way, we point out opportunities and elaborate on our options.

❏ 4

Our World

Are We Entering a Depression in the 1990s?

"The process of gathering knowledge does not lead to knowing. An answer is inevitably the parent of a great family of new questions. So we draw worlds and fit them against the world about us, and crumple them when they do not fit, and draw new ones."

John Steinbeck

Undoubtedly there are some similarities between the 1920s and 1980s. The sequence of business developments in these two decades indicates that we should carefully assess our future options. In light of these similarities, *can a depression take place in the 1990s?*

Before we draw conclusions, we ought to examine the *differences* between the twenties and the eighties. There have been radical economic, social, structural, and international changes over the past 60 years. A study of the world's cross-currents should help us to understand better the juncture we are at. In this chapter, we will study some of the changes that have evolved over the past 60 years on both the international and domestic fronts. We will also analyze some of the factors that could have a significant influence on our future.

One of the most important factors is that today we have a better understanding of the economic policies that could prevent the recurrence of the painful thirties—and many of these policies are already in force. The New Deal paved the way for government involvement in business; now the government can use all of its power to prevent the replay of the Great Depression. In the past four decades, government policies managed to bring about healthy economic growth. Since World War II, government strategies have been successfully directed at supporting businesses that appear to be promising. The fundamental question is: Can these policies be as effective during times of severe adjustments as they have proven to be during prosperity? If we capitalize on our knowledge of the world around us, we could see our way to safe shores.

A GLOBAL INTERDEPENDENCE

There are significant differences between the twenties and the eighties in the international economic and political arena. Since the Great Depression, the world has grown more interdependent. With the rise of multinational companies, global trading exploded, accompanied by radical improvements in the communication of information and statistics and in technological transfer. Over the course of recent decades, reductions in the cost of telecommunications among nations have led to the proliferation of information. The commercialization of airplanes since the twenties has revolutionized transportation around the world and has facilitated both trading and labor mobility among nations. In addition, the flow of international assets has increased. Direct investments grew, which helped the transfer of technology around the globe. Today, manufactured goods represent a large portion of world trade.

The explosion in world trade over the past three decades has, in turn, led to an increase in the exchange of both capital and financial assets. Global financial markets proliferated, and careful coordination of economic policies among nations became crucial. The stability of the world economy today depends on the synchronization of those policies among both developed and developing nations. Consequently, the world has grown more sensitive to imbalances around the globe.

The General Agreement for Tariffs and Trade (GATT) was drawn up to prevent the recurrence of the "beggar thy neighbor" policies of the thirties. The wide-open and growing world market gave rise to the progressive nations of the Far East. Japan soared as an international competitor and established itself as an economic giant. Newly industrialized countries (NICs), such as South Korea, Taiwan, Hong Kong, and Singapore, also rose during the past decade. Brazil, Mexico, and others likewise gained ground in the international economy and made strides toward developing their industrial base.

The world's population has more than doubled over the past 60 years, with most of the gains in Africa, Asia, and South America. In those very same economies, people have been relying on depletable natural resources. The majority of those countries are classified as low income, low technology, and low growth. They have been in a constant struggle to build economies that can compete with industrialized countries. Although they admire Western civilization for the wealth it has created for its own people, very few of the less developed countries (LDCs) abide by the rules of the free enterprise. Dictatorships or heavy government intervention characterizes their internal business affairs.

The socialist countries of the 1920s comprised only about 9 percent of the world population; since then they have risen to well over 35 percent. The emergence of the two world superpowers that followed World War II marked the beginning of political tension on a global scale. Efforts to limit the mushrooming of a centrally planned economy and socialism have led to more direct communication between the haves and the have-nots. The free Western democracies have been trying to win the support or at least the neutrality of the less economically developed nations, which, in turn, has given those lower-income countries a voice in world affairs. These efforts have also imposed on the Western allies the responsibility of increasing their aid and loans to these developing economies. Moreover, coordination of economic policies became crucial in order to prevent the LDCs from falling under communism.

The increase of global economic interdependence and concern for the poverty of Third World countries have led to the proliferation of international organizations, such as the World Bank, the International Monetary Fund, the Economic and Social Council of the United Nations, and the European Economic Community. These organizations and others help smooth out the development process of the global economy. They provide developing nations with monetary help, training programs, or administrative assistance. They also contribute toward global understanding and serve as a link between the industrialized and developing nations.

THE DANGEROUS YEARS ... THE SEVENTIES

The seventies witnessed economic shocks not seen since the onset of the twentieth century. During the seventies, there were many significant developments that had a major impact on the world as well as on the domestic economy.

First, the baby boomers of World War II rushed to the marketplace and consumed everything in sight. They flooded the job market with their modest experience, tasted the ultimate in human knowledge, and helped take the age of supertechnology to an ever-greener horizon.

Moreover, the flood of women to the job market marked the beginning of a new era: an era in which women took their place as an integral part of the economy. Women will continue to contribute their share to our future growth. They have already taken their place in the executive suite, built businesses, and revolutionized the workplace. Not only in the United States, but in Japan, Europe, and most countries around the world, women are increasingly joining the labor force. In the long term, this could stimulate growth and add to the world's economic pie.

At the highest pedestal of civilization, we could not escape our responsibilities to provide a pollution-free environment for our people and future generations. We bore the brunt of added costs of pollution control, which led to squeezed profits and lower productivity. Several industrial sectors were caught off guard, earnings of major corporations plummeted, and unemployment soared to levels that had not been seen since the Great Depression.

During the same decade, the mightiest of all cartels in the history of mankind was born. The Arabs got together to control the price of the most vital natural resource to modern civilization. The Oil-Producing Export Countries (OPEC) influenced the world growth curve with their oil-pricing decisions. Both industrial and developing nations had to bear the brunt of the oil shocks. In real terms, global economic growth almost came to a grinding halt. In fact, the progress of several energy-poor countries, which had to absorb the sudden price increase of that vital commodity, was halted. International trade deficits showed their ugly faces in the balances of payments of most countries. Wealth was shifted to the fat accounts of OPEC.

A recycling of those surpluses back to developing nations became a priority. American banks assumed that responsibility and loaned large sums to Third World countries. In the eighties, declining prices and a shrinking economic pie made those same debts the time bombs that threaten disastrous loan defaults.

The Japanese invasion of the world market also began in the seventies. They sold watches, televisions, cars, and any other technological innovation conceivable. They became associated with quality and efficient manufacturing, and their balance of payments grew richer at the expense of every nation on the face of the earth. The world became fascinated with the business management and phenomenal growth of the Japanese, who were considered the hottest case study in business schools. They took over the world arena, dislocated the industrial structure of the West, and crippled LDCs' chances to compete in the global economy. They caused friction in the marketplace and threatened the existence of entire industries around the world.

The process of globalization of the world's economy accelerated. Inflation was rampant in industrialized as well as industrializing nations. The East, the West, the North, and the South all had to come to a better understanding to prevent the economic slowdown from turning into a collapse. In the United States, the inflation of the seventies made interest rates soar to their highest level in the century. It also prompted a major shift in investment portfolios to real assets. A flight to the safe havens of real estate led to excessive speculation in that vital sector of the economy. In addition, the subdued stock market of the seventies made corporations borrow money from banks at an exorbitant cost, instead of issuing equities at depressed prices.

THE MISUNDERSTOOD STAGFLATION

In the seventies, our economy suffered from "stagflation," which is high inflation and high unemployment occurring at the same time. Stagflation became the talk of cocktail parties, but was often misunderstood. Economists were baffled by the simultaneous rise of both inflation and unemployment. The administrators' confusion about its origin led them to concentrate on fighting inflation alone. They resorted to stringent monetary policies that pushed interest rates to unprecedented heights. Meanwhile, experts cited the oil shocks, the extra burden of pollution control, shortages on the supply side, and declines in productivity as possible reasons for stagflation.

However, one of the least addressed factors—and probably the most important—was demographics. The baby boomers were a major force behind the puzzling behavior of the economy of the seventies. When they flooded the job market, they exercised pressure on both prices and employment prospects.

As they earned decent incomes, they went on buying sprees. The demand for all sorts of goods climbed. Business did not anticipate that sudden surge in demand, and production capacity was expanding slowly. Pressures on prices mounted and led to high inflation. Moreover, as the baby boomers formed families, they wanted to own homes. This, in turn, created a sudden demand for housing, which further intensified the rise of inflation.

Moreover, as the baby boomers entered the job market in large numbers, unemployment started to rise simultaneously with inflation. The number of jobs available could not expand to keep up with the rate of their entrance into the labor force. Thus, crowding of the labor market pushed unemployment higher, and demand for consumption led to inflation.

Basic courses of economics preach three determinants of vital importance to the future prospect of economic growth, namely labor, land, and capital. Land is abundant, and capital is influenced by investment opportunities that depend on consumption. Consumption is a function of the size of the population and the standard of living. The labor force and the income per household determine the growth of demand for goods. As the baby boomers account for about 50 percent of the labor force, they are a force to be reckoned with in this economic system of balances.

A BULGE WAS BORN

Census Bureau statistics indicate that the baby boom officially began in the mid-1940s. Substantial gains in the number of newborn babies continued into the early 1960s. The mothers that bore those babies were born during the twenties and the thirties. Their husbands, too, were born during that time. The marriage rate, which was high during those days, reached a peak of about 96 percent during the 1930s.

Explanations for the baby boom phenomenon range from a high fertility rate to the family's rise of importance as the nucleus of society. The war pulled the economy out of the

Great Depression, and good times were back again. However, the psychology of the forties still held onto the sentimental values that dominated the depression years. The process of rebuilding the world after the destruction of the war was at its best. With the broad recovery and solid growth, the environment was ripe for a substantial increase in population.

THEY RESHAPED THE WORLD

In the 1950s, baby boomers flooded schools and caused unprecedented growth in the educational system. The richest nation in the world was going through a transitional stage of explosive expansion in education, wealth, and technical advancement.

In the 1960s, the baby boomers let their hair grow, played loud music, loved the Beatles, and said no to Vietnam. They rushed to Woodstock and rode motorcycles. Motorcycle gangs and easy riders were symbols of their attitude toward life. Miniskirts came in vogue, coinciding with the go-go years of the stock market. The baby boomers entered the job market in the early sixties when they officially reached the working age. Teenagers, the fastest-growing segment of the population, entered the labor force. As fast as the resilient economy could absorb them, new teenagers kept coming. Unemployment among teenagers was an ever-increasing trend as the invasion of the job market continued unabated.

In the seventies, the baby boomers reached the age of responsibility. They cut their hair short, and the Harvard look grew popular. They earned a decent living, bought houses, and unleashed their savvy appetite for consumption that the rich markets afforded them. They took the economy hostage—as the supply of products and goods fell behind their hungry dollars. Moreover, imports increased at a faster pace. With the energy shortage, the baby boomers demanded more energy-efficient cars and bought Hondas.

Statistics indicate that the economy added some 30 million new entrants to the job market between 1965 and 1980.

Employment became tight, and industries could hardly continue to absorb those massive numbers of job seekers. Strains in the economy began to show in official statistical reports.

The baby boomers earned more than previous generations. Their large number led to intense competition. In the sixties and seventies, their inexperience contributed to declining productivity. In the 1980s, competition for top jobs grew more intense as many among them vied for key slots.

The baby boomers' pressure on the housing market was particularly pronounced as prices skyrocketed. As baby boomers formed families, they demanded more houses than ever before. The world of plenty, changing cultural values, the growing sense of independence, and the shrinking capacity for human tolerance led to frustration and divorce. In turn, more adults chose to live alone, which led to a greater need for houses. The expanding demand, combined with the psychological perception of future inflation, fueled the huge jump in prices of real estate.

The fast increase in prices spread throughout the economy. The perception of continuing inflation, combined with a relatively slower rate of increase in personal income compared with the overall price structure of the economy, gave way to lower savings rates. However, with two persons earning income in the family, a sense of security prevailed.

BABY BOOMERS IN CORPORATE AMERICA

In the 1980s, the baby boomers constitute slightly more than half of the labor force. They reshaped corporate cultures and are pushing for more power. They are pro-growth, pro-deregulation, pro-environment, and pro-abortion. They are better educated, extremely ambitious, conservative liberals. They are against big defense spending and have little corporate loyalty.

They invaded corporate America with new ideals and values. In the corporate environment, they advocate participatory decision making, quality circles, the team spirit, entrepreneurship, and autonomy. They took over the top management of several corporations and reshaped their market strategies. The record of their success at Burger King demonstrated the effectiveness of their changes, which challenged the dominance of McDonald's. They built Compaq and dared to challenge IBM. They sought refuge from traditional business practices and rode the bandwagon of supertechnology. They created Microsoft, Apple Computers, Ashton Tate, Lotus Development, and many other companies that revolutionized our lives at home and in the office. And their ability to use sophisticated computers matched their predecessors' comfort with pens and pencils.

This has led to a clash between the baby boomers and traditional corporate America. The hippies of yesteryear invaded the alleys of academia and earned more MBAs than their predecessors. They are intensely competitive and frustrated with the limited upward mobility that most firms offer them. Their dreams and ambitions are encountering resistance from the old-fashioned organizations of their fathers. Tension between the two generations has mounted. Those at the top adhere to traditional methods of promotion through long corporate loyalty; the boomers, on the other hand, are a part of fast-track America. Some companies, recognizing their motivations, devised dual career paths. Incentive compensation policies were adopted by many corporations to encourage the creative spirit of the baby boomers.

The baby boomers command substantial voting power and could effect a change in the balance of electoral ballots. The real struggle lies ahead, as this class struggle will heat up later in this century. A population that is growing older could impose further strains on the socioeconomic structure as they advance toward the ever-appealing stage of politics.

The baby boomers are faced with the challenge of the generation, and in their hands rests the solution that can reinforce leadership in America. They could tilt the balance of power in the international arena by quenching their appetite for imported products. They are the administrators of tomorrow and the policy makers of the future. They are the most highly skilled labor force in the history of mankind. At their knees lie the forces of change that could save the world from the prophecies of the Siberian killer wave.

As the 1980s and 1990s unfold, the baby boomers will face yet more challenging decisions. Automation and robotization of the factory will surface as a debate of social responsibility toward coming generations. Who gets what and how can our society effectively deal with the distribution of wealth? What decisions will the baby boomers finally make?

They have already freed entrepreneurship from its limited definition and taken us toward new promising horizons. They hold the keys to our future economic growth, and they can bring America back to the path of competitiveness. They are the hope of the next century and the leaders that will guide us through the coming industrial renaissance. How they are going to choose to shape the world is yet to be seen. But they hold the answer to many key questions that will continue to affect the world long after they leave the scene.

IT'S A WOMAN'S WORLD TOO

One of the most significant social and economic changes of the past 60 years is the entrance of women into the job market. They represent more than 54 percent of the labor force and account for two-thirds of its increase in the seventies.

Doors have opened for women in every walk of life. In the past decade, women flooded the service sector and held low-paid jobs. However, recently, they have succeeded in every field of endeavor and have knocked on the door of the executive suite. In the eighties, a woman held a position on the U.S. Supreme Court, another was nominated as a vice presidential candidate for the White House, and yet another represented the United States at the United Nations. They became astronauts, brokers, engineers, accountants, business executives, and investment bankers. They proved to the world that they can—and will—continue to contribute to the future of the global economy. They account for over one-third of the new startup companies each year in the United States and have already demonstrated their potential as entrepreneurs.

The women's movement is an irreversible fundamental change. In the twenties, women were a wasted resource that society did not use to enhance growth. In the seventies and eighties, women increased the purchasing power per household. Their entrance into the job market coincided with the fast growth of the service sector, which facilitated their integration into the labor force. The number of women earning higher education degrees is growing, and their skills in the business world have increased.

The women's movement has far-reaching social implications. The birth rate has declined, and there is an ever-growing need for day-care centers for children. Families today have fewer members. The time spent at home has shrunk, and living habits have changed. Eating out has given rise to a proliferation of fast food restaurants. The need for a more efficient way to spend time at home revolutionized the modern kitchen and living room. Today, more families are using the microwave to cook, and ready-made meals to cut the time of preparing food. The need for entertainment after a long day of work is also on the rise. Shopping via TV programs is gaining popularity, and catalog businesses have been booming. The lack of time spent with children puts a heavier burden on our schools and educational institutions.

However, the most important social implication is the substantial drop in newborn babies, which implies a corresponding drop in future entrants into the job market. Some experts are already talking about the future shortage in the labor force after the baby boom generation retires. While this may be accurate, the future automation of manufacturing and service may allow for the preservation of levels of output without increasing the labor force. As a matter of fact, this drop may help raise the standard of living for the next generation, as resources will be shared by a smaller number of people.

Women in America were able to expand their horizons from being housewives and homemakers to professionals of the highest potential and esteem. They came from every walk of life to serve their countries, their families, and their institutions. For our future generations, they should continue to stand side by side with the capable men of their choice to help keep the dream of the great United States alive. For that we salute the most welcomed revolution of our time.

THE COST OF CIVILIZATION

The Health and Safety Act, which was enacted in 1969, completely changed traditional methods of manufacturing. The environmental revolution asserted itself at the turn of the 1970s. Leading the universe to the promising land of tomorrow, we assumed our responsibility to leave to our future generations a pollution-free environment. The Occupational Safety and Health Administration (OSHA) was inaugurated and policed the industrial society with an iron fist. Over the years, we made progress toward reducing the hazards of pollution, but the cost to the economy was high.

Productivity, which began to decline in the mid-sixties, took a tumble. Industry after industry faced severe constraints on their traditional methods of production. However, the cost of environmental control was not shared equally by all industries. The electronic and high tech companies hardly felt its burden. Others, such as utilities, steel, chemicals, and the automobile industry, were hard hit. Many utility companies shifted from coal, which emits sulfur dioxide, to low sulfur oil derived from refining imported oil. Catalytic converters found their way into 1975 car models to reduce hydrocarbons, nitrogen oxides, and carbon monoxide.

In sum, smokestack corporations were seriously hit with the heavy burden of restrictive emission standards. The cost of production per employee rose, and profit margins were squeezed. The demand for pollution control equipment soared. The companies supplying goods and products to reduce air pollution prospered: A whole new industry was born.

Our demands for a pollution-free environment coincided with the first flood of baby boomers joining the productive labor force of our nation. This led to an imbalance on the supply side—we were replacing old manufacturing equipment while demand was increasing at a faster pace. Efforts were spent complying with environmental constraints rather than expanding the supply of goods; companies were too busy meeting the pollution challenge and replacing existing machinery to increase their production capacity. This additional burden ultimately increased the pressure on inflation and led to the precipitous slide of productivity.

While the older industries in the United States were scrambling to meet the challenge of a new wave of pollution control, young Japanese companies were gearing up for intense competition. In the sixties and early seventies, Japanese companies were blessed by the opportunity to build their modern production facilities with an adequate level of pollution control. This stroke of luck went unnoticed by many observers evaluating the reasons behind Japan's success in capturing a decent share of the U.S. market.

The President's Council on Environmental Control released a study in 1974, which admitted that environmental programs contributed about 0.5 percent to inflation. They consumed 1 percent of our Gross National Product (GNP). They also constituted 2–3 percent of all investment expenditures and 5–6 percent of total expenditures on industrial plant and equipment. Those numbers were expected to increase as the seventies proceeded. In the eighties, the trend continued unabated in the form of waste management, reclamation of solid and liquid waste, and recycling of metals, trash, and garbage to produce energy.

Basically, we had to pay the price for civilization. We had to provide our people with a better quality of life. We exercised our responsibility to leave future generations with a heritage of which they will be proud. No one can debate the critical need for us to improve the quality of life on earth and to preserve nature from our industrial pollution. However, *the timing of that environmental revolution came at the worst possible moment. We had to bear these costs as we simultaneously faced the challenges of soaring consumption, the oil shocks, and the Japanese economic invasion.*

Nevertheless, we rid our environment of pollution and moved quickly toward dealing with new economic challenges. The bulk of the cost of environmental control is now behind us. The future seems to hold the promise of full automation in manufacturing. In the future, new facilities could be installed with much lower levels of pollution. These improvements could be a one-time charge to our productivity and national wealth, unless we insist on pushing toward the elusive point of zero discharge. If that were to happen, costs would escalate sharply and further resources would be spent on a goal that is not justified by the incremental benefit derived from it.

HOW HAVE WE CHANGED SINCE THE TWENTIES?

The economy of the eighties is totally different from that of the twenties. Over the past 60 years, there has been a radical shift among the sectors of the economy that provide employment. First, there has been a smooth transition from an agrarian economy to an industrial one. In the early twenties, agriculture provided a little over 30 percent of jobs in the economy. By 1929, only about 21 percent of the labor force still worked in agriculture. In the eighties, that percentage declined further to around 3 percent of the total labor force.

From 1920 to the early 1950s, the industrial sector kept expanding its role as the provider of a larger percentage of work in the economy. Since the early 1960s, the trend toward automation and overseas manufacturing accelerated, and employment in manufacturing began to decline. The percentage of employees in manufacturing shrank from over 30 percent in the early sixties to less than 20 percent in the mid-eighties.

During the seventies and eighties, the service sector has been able to absorb a flood of new entrants into the job market. There has been healthy growth in several industries that are service oriented, such as restaurants, telecommunications, air travel, banking, insurance, and brokerage. The service sector in the eighties provides employment to well over 60 percent of the total labor force. This indicates to us that the postindustrial society is well upon us.

While the contribution of the agricultural sector has declined, the output of the farm has substantially increased since the twenties. Today, we simply rely less on the human factor to produce our agricultural needs. Called "vertical integration," this process uses machinery to achieve much more efficient production.

Along the same lines, automation has gradually been replacing factory workers. Here again, the vertical integration of manufacturing is leading us quickly toward the fully automated factory of the future. This does not mean that manufactured products will disappear and that we will import all our needs from abroad. In both cases, what we are in fact witnessing is a step forward toward tomorrow's world of abundance.

Another major difference between the economies of the eighties and the twenties is that the skill of the labor force has leaped forward. The percentage of the labor force with basic and higher education has increased dramatically. We live today in the age of supercomputers and the frontiers of the most advanced technology that man has ever known. Genetic engineering, wonder drugs, flexible manufacturing, and space technology are taking us to horizons that even optimists in the twenties could hardly envision.

The government's share of the economy has also expanded. The total federal government's expenditures in 1929 were about 9 percent of GNP, including defense spending. In 1939, just before World War II, defense spending amounted to about 1.3 percent of GNP. In 1986, defense expenditures constituted about 6.7 percent of GNP, and total government expenditures well exceeded 20 percent of GNP. The participation of the government in the economy has substantially increased since the twenties. This increase in the relative size and participation of the government has a cushioning effect on the overall economy. It tends to add stability to the aggregate market for goods and services.

Moreover, the transfer of payments outlay was negligible in the twenties compared to what it is today. The reallocation of national resources to provide state and local aid, entitlement programs for the elderly, social welfare, and unemployment compensation adds a further cushion to dampen the effects of a severe downswing in the economy.

The depression of the thirties witnessed a severe shrinkage in consumption. Unemployment compensation did not exist; instead, relief programs were implemented during the New Deal to stimulate demand and to stop the deflation in prices. Even the 1974–1975 global recession, which was referred to as the most devastating economic slowdown since the Great Depression, did not come close to the decline in real economic aggregates during the thirties. The government today could take any measures necessary and intervene in the marketplace to halt a downward economic slide.

The proliferation of economic data in the eighties also sets us apart from the twenties. The statistical gathering methods and the speed of information available to our monetary authorities could not be matched by the fragmented—and sometimes even incorrect—data that were used in the twenties. The interpretation of these data has likewise advanced. In the twenties, the basis of fiscal policy and its stimulating effects on the economy were not understood. The Keynesian theory, stipulating that government spending bails out the economy during periods of severe economic downturns, was not popular during the twenties. Keynes himself tried to convince Roosevelt of its merits amid the calamity of those days. Moreover, monetary policies and methods of measuring monetary aggregates today could not be compared with the primitive understanding of the twenties.

In light of these facts, when we examine the investment arena and the crash of 1987, we do not detect the speculative orgy of the twenties. In the eighties, major portions of investment portfolios are not concentrated only in equities, but in fixed income securities. Bond portfolios are much larger than they were in the twenties.

To the naked eye, the great bull market of the eighties appeared to be the greatest bull market of the century. Yet, if we look beyond the obvious, we realize that this is not true. When adjusted for the inflation that developed since 1913, the market has not surpassed its peak scored in 1929. Despite the fascinating growth of corporate America, the market at its ultimate high in 1987 failed to account for the years of expansion and sophistication that our companies acquired. In addition, if we adjust it to the depreciation in the purchasing power of our devalued dollar, we can conclude that securities today are cheap and reasonably valued. This leads us to wonder whether we have already seen the greatest bull market of our time or whether that dream is still ahead of us.

In sum, a statistical comparison between the twenties and the eighties encounters major differences in the overall structure of the different sectors of the economy.

A BLESSING IN DISGUISE ... THE FALTERING DOLLAR

A very important difference between the twenties and the eighties is the currency float. The fluctuation of the dollar in the foreign exchange market has a direct impact on the course of business. It acts as a balancing mechanism for the global economy.

In the early eighties, well after the inflation of the seventies subsided, the Federal Reserve Board (FED) kept real interest rates high. From 1980 to 1985, the dollar rose substantially in the foreign exchange market. We celebrated the strength of our currency, although it caused our industrial base to suffer. Imports soared and the trade deficit ballooned. The Japanese got rich at our expense and started telling us how superior their management techniques were. For a while, some among us believed them.

At that point, corporate America had to map out a counterstrategy to compete worldwide. The better of two evils was to manufacture overseas in countries that could provide cheaper labor. This, in turn, precipitated the decline of our industrial base and led to the hollowing of our corporations. Jobs were taken away from the domestic economy and travelled to far-off lands.

We had no other choice in the face of savvy foreign competition and a strong dollar. The last thing we wanted to do was to close our markets to exports. Ours were the first signatures on the GATT; in fact, we are the leaders of free trade. The dollar simply had to adjust to the new realities of international trade. It required boldness on the part of our leaders and the FED to let the dollar decline without intervening. For a short while, we had to sacrifice our pride and let the massacre of our greenback take place.

The dollar's decline will revive our long-lost competitiveness and welcome manufacturing back to America. It is a process—not an event—and should take several years to yield desired benefits. The dollar's decline will make our products more competitive in the global market, which will help shift manufacturing back to the United States. It should also sharply curtail the Japanese invasion of the world market and put a dent in their aggressive export strategies. The soaring yen has already shocked the Japanese economy. For a change, they may have to taste the bitterness of industrial decline, which they once forced on the rest of the world.

One drawback of the temporary weakness of the dollar is that America is cheap and may be up for sale. Our lands and buildings in major cities are bargains for foreigners, after accounting for currency translation. Our companies, stocks, and bonds are at rock-bottom prices considering their book value and intrinsic worth. They may remain bargains while reindustrialization proceeds on course and while debt liquidation takes its toll on the economy. But once this process is complete, we will look back at the temporary weakness of our dollar and say that it was the better of two evils.

ARE WE ENTERING ANOTHER GREAT DEPRESSION?

A depression of the magnitude of the thirties is highly unlikely to occur today. But a severe prolonged adjustment is possible. We cannot conceive of a decline in real economic activity in the years ahead that could even come close to the devastating numbers that we detailed in our discussion of the Great Depression. However, we have a number of challenges to deal with if we are to regain our declining standard of living.

First, there is the challenge of surmounting the debt burden, which has reached alarming proportions at the government, corporate, and consumer levels. The extended real estate sector could experience a serious adjustment in the early nineties, which could entail a slowdown in that vital sector of the economy. Clearly, we have lived beyond our means, and the process of debt liquidation has to be handled with the utmost care if we are to prevent it from becoming painful.

We also face the challenge of taking on the Japanese invasion of the world market. We have to gear up for the competitive world ahead of us and revitalize our manufacturing base. Careful planning and preparation for the factories of the future should lead to retraining of displaced workers from dying industries. Automation in manufacturing will challenge our educational institutions, which will have to develop courses necessary to upgrade the skills of the labor force to cope with fast-moving technology.

We have lost our place as the unchallenged leaders in competitiveness and in productivity. Our trade deficit is an indication of our declining industrial superiority. Over the past 60 years we have turned from the largest creditor nation into the largest debtor nation in the world. It is time to revitalize our manufacturing base and regain our competitiveness in the international as well as the domestic markets. We cannot rely on the service sector to bring back our faltering standard of living and our past economic superiority.

The challenge of targeting our research and development toward finding solutions that stimulate growth also lies ahead. We also have to find ways to protect our patents from being copied by industrial espionage.

The challenges ahead are many, and there are many options to choose from. We have to heed the stock market crash of 1987, which signalled an important message. We have to leave complacency behind and work toward solutions. The deterioration in the domestic and international economies has reached a critical stage. We have to be careful for many years to come if we look forward to a soft landing for our economic problems. Fortunately, the baby boomers are here in their best productive years. They represent a power that has never been available to the economy; they are highly trained, highly skilled, and highly motivated. They represent the hope for the next generation.

☐ 5

Boom or Bust

Real Estate in America

"To everything there is a season, and a time to every purpose under the heaven: A time to be born, and a time to die; a time to plant, and a time to pluck up that which is planted; a time to get, and a time to lose; a time to keep, and a time to cast away..."

The Book of Ecclesiastes

The greatest of all books tells us that life on earth goes through cycles. Prosperity does not last forever; good times are followed by bad times. In the free enterprise economy, nothing is more true than this simple fact. Expansion is followed by contraction of business activities; cycles of boom are followed by periods of adjustments that rid the system of accumulated excesses. This has happened throughout history and will happen again in the future. But those who live within their means fare well when business is sluggish. Those who think that nothing can go wrong end up suffering painful consequences when bad times hit. As a matter of fact, in Chinese, the word crisis is represented by two symbols: danger and opportunity.

While the world is structurally different today than that which existed earlier in this century, there are some pitfalls that we have to be aware of. While a replay of the thirties is unlikely, housing market activities stand at the center of what the future could hold.

One of the major sectors in the domestic economy is real estate, which is no exception to these truisms. Buying a house constitutes the single largest investment that most people ever make in their lifetime. When a house is bought, furniture has to be purchased. Appliances are also important in a modern house. A new homeowner probably has to acquire a second car as well. Kitchen utensils, rugs, gardening equipment, electronic devices, and security systems are necessities that also go with buying a house.

Because of these interconnections, a slowdown in the real estate market would have a considerable impact on the economy. It would lead to a marked decline in the consumption of an array of other commodities and goods that are highly dependent on the housing market. Indeed, the repercussions of a soft real estate market could affect almost all other industries in the economy.

Like any other market, the vital real estate sector may go through an adjustment. Yet, this may represent a great opportunity for those who are not overextended. Over the years, real estate has proven to be the best hedge against inflation. During periods of a business slowdown, real estate does not stand to lose a large percentage of its worth, as equities and other investment vehicles do.

THE DREAM OF A LIFETIME

In this country, real estate is not only the privilege of the rich, as it is in other parts of the world. Buying a house to raise a family is an integral part of the promise of the free enterprise economy.

In the past few years, real estate prices have appreciated substantially in the housing market. People saw the value of their real estate tripling and even quadrupling in some cases. The demand for houses, condominiums, and cooperatives soared. In the early eighties, properties appreciated at a much faster rate than did any other investment. This surge in demand was due to several factors, detailed below.

In the seventies, inflation swept the nation and propelled a huge rise in the prices of real assets. To protect their net worth, families rushed to the housing market.

The baby boomers of the post-World War II era were beginning to raise families. As the economy absorbed them into the job market, they earned decent incomes, which enabled them to settle down in places of their own. Inflation's presence, which boosted the already rising prices, convinced them even more of the necessity of acquiring their first house as soon as possible. Their motivation to buy came initially as a natural stage of their independence.

In addition, the evolution of the two-paycheck society boosted the family's available spending power. Income per household—with two members earning wages—rose substantially. This increase in family income eased the burden of servicing mortgage debt. This newly found wealth helped to enhance the standard of living in real terms, as it initially compensated for the decline in purchasing power that resulted from inflation. This additional salary earned per household also added to the sense of security: If one of the two working partners were to lose his or her job, the income generated by the other was sufficient to meet mortgage payments.

Another trend that began during the sixties and accelerated in the seventies was an increased number of divorces and single heads of households. This further contributed to the demand for housing. In sum, a larger number of houses were being purchased by a young and prosperous generation.

Another important factor that contributed to the real estate market boom in the seventies was the emerging service sector. The service sector continued to expand, absorbing the new entrants into the job market. The Japanese invasion of U.S. markets was taking its toll on the manufacturing sector, which began to shrink. Meanwhile, the service sector was filling the employment gap that the manufacturing sector left. Gains from the service sector helped to provide families with additional income to support the demand for real estate and also boosted demand for office buildings.

Interest rates were low in real terms and trailed inflation during most of the seventies. The stock market was not enticing and did not present a viable alternative for preserving the purchasing power of money earned. So, investors flocked to the real estate market as a safe and secure investment that did not seem to abate. Despite the phenomenal rise of interest rates in the early eighties, the sharp advance in real estate prices enhanced real estate's appeal.

The higher inflation rose, the more people expected it to continue on its upward course. This perception further increased real estate demand, which, in turn, maintained the price rise in the housing market. And the more real estate prices advanced, the more confident investors became about future price appreciation.

The speculative fever became deeply ingrained into people's psychology and drove them to assume more risk. Those who owned a house moved to a bigger one and assumed a little more debt. Those who had already paid the mortgage on their homes borrowed against their equity to invest in a more expensive home. As interest rates began to precipitously decline, buyers looked for a second chance to participate in these bargains. Prices, meanwhile, continued their advance in both high- and low-interest-rate environments.

The real estate sections of major newspapers expanded. Brokerage firms, banks, and savings and loan associations crowded the market and extended loans to prospective buyers. Everybody was happy—from the owners to the renters to the financiers who afforded mortgages to buyers.

When a powerful trend of speculation and euphoria develops in a particular market, you do not have to be smart or astute to realize phenomenal gains. This was the case in the real estate sector during the boom years. Apartment dwellers who were living peacefully in their buildings were suddenly presented with a great opportunity to become rich. Every building that went cooperative or that was converted into condominiums offered tenants a windfall profit that multiplied their net worth almost overnight. In the great majority of cases, the inside price was substantially lower than the market price. Tenants did not even have to tie up the down payment for a long time: There were plenty of buyers waiting to purchase their property at a much higher price, giving them a handsome profit. A phony sense of richness prevailed, as buyers saw the values of their real estate rise in an uninterrupted course. The late seventies and the early eighties, in particular, brought fortunes made in the real estate market beyond the wildest dreams to the average household.

History tells us that no nation has ever had its entire population made up of millionaires without incurring an adjustment. Yet, for a while, the housing market of the seventies and eighties held that promise. In real life, of course, such a concept is self-defeating; if everybody is rich, the desire to produce or even to work at all vanishes. People will want to spend more time on leisure activities alone.

THE ROTATION OF PROSPERITY

At its early stages, the real estate boom was not evenly spread throughout every state. It started in the West and the Midwest. In the early seventies, the price of farmlands in the agricultural sector began to rise above that of the rest of the country. Stories of multimillionaire farmers making it in real estate were everywhere in the business sections of daily newspapers.

Meanwhile, the great service society, which was acclaimed to be the provider of future business growth, was leaping forward. In Dallas, Denver, Los Angeles, and other major cities around the nation, new fancy office buildings were erected to meet the demands of the growing service sector. According to the National Association of Realtors, investment in nonresidential buildings exceeded $1 trillion between 1978 and 1986.

California and its neighboring states were among the first geographic areas to benefit from this boom. Unbelievable price appreciation materialized in that part of the country and led the way to the great land boom. Next came the Sunbelt states;

we were told that Texas was the fastest-growing place in the nation. Blessed with abundant oil reserves in a world hungry for that most vital commodity, real estate had to boom in that part of the country.

The Northeast was the last area to taste the riches of the real estate boom. New York City and its vicinity caught up with the explosive price rise during the first half of the 1980s. Not only did the prestigious neighborhoods of the Big Apple see huge price advances, but the slums of New York also had their share. Parts of the city that were once completely written off by real estate developers witnessed the most intense speculative price appreciation seen in the last few decades.

On the borders of New York City, Long Island was suddenly rediscovered as the new home of growing prosperity. The rush to Long Island allowed the average family to own a dream house. During the first half of the eighties, Long Island saw the biggest appreciation in real estate values ever remembered.

IT FUELED THE TAKEOVER MANIA ON WALL STREET

Companies' real estate divisions were ranked among the most profitable contributors to their bottom-line earnings. Some companies incurred losses on their main lines of business but yielded handsome gains from their real estate holdings. The stock market was slow to reflect the intrinsic worth of corporations when their real estate holdings appreciated.

However, this tremendous appreciation of corporate real estate value triggered the takeover mania on Wall Street. The term "asset strippers" found its way into the stock market when undervalued equities of the late seventies and early eighties were subjected to one of the wildest waves of corporate takeovers in history.

The acquirer established a sizable position in the targeted company. Soon after, a tender offer above the market price was announced to shareholders. The company was then either merged into another entity or taken private. Later, the

acquirer sold the real estate holdings at a handsome profit—
several times more than what he or she paid for buying out
the company. Once the assets were stripped, the acquired
company was either consolidated into a subsidiary of the
acquirer or sold to another company. If no buyer existed, the
company could always be put back on the market in the form
of a new issue or in any other way that the geniuses of finance
could devise.

THE COLOR OF SPECULATION

The history of speculative bubbles indicates a common
pattern to their development. They usually begin and progress
in a slow and unnoticed way. They stay on course for a long
time, well after several predictions of their demise have been
made by gurus of the time. The fact that they soar beyond
wildest expectations creates a hypnotic sense of continuity and
eternity. At the final stage of their advance—the most vicious
of them all—people are totally convinced that their continua-
tion is assured. "This time it is different..." becomes the conviction of all observers. Justification of the rise finds many
volunteers. Who dares to disagree, especially when confronted with the strength of the logic of those who made it in
those markets?

In most cases, you stand to make great profits as long as
you leave some money on the table and control your appetite
for the last dollar you can get. All speculative fevers, such as
the North Sea bubble, the Florida real estate bonanza of the
mid-twenties, the stock market bulge of 1929, the go-go years
of the 1960s, rises of the prices of gold and silver in the late
1970s, and OPEC's unbelievable hike in the price of oil in
1973–1974 have the same characteristics.

When waves of speculation reach their turning point,
they do not ring a bell—and they do not hesitate either. They
plummet and continue to do so without allowing for an exit.
Just as they exaggerated their advance, they proceed with a
vengeance to downside extremes. They are painful and unre-

lenting. Before they end, it is usually difficult to anticipate what will bring about their final halt.

Consider, for example, OPEC and the oil shocks. Oil is Western civilization's most vital source of energy. However, it skyrocketed in price in the mid-seventies, until we thought that $15 per barrel was the end of the painful price advance. Soon, it proved to be only a pause before another jump carried the price to $30 per barrel. The threat to modern civilization became real. Not only did the long lines of automobiles at gas pumps remind us of our vulnerability, but corporate planning and pension allocation became very difficult to account for. The rising course of oil prices continued in a vicious spiral of price escalation. It seemed, for a while, as if there were no end in sight to OPEC's control of our lives. Even optimists expected only a modest pause before oil prices proceeded to ever-higher grounds. One could not envision why prices should come down at all. After all, modern civilization depends on that commodity. Even if supply were to exceed demand, experts maintained, the mighty cartel would cut its production and thereby prevent prices from declining.

However, measures of conservation began to take place. We got rid of the old gas guzzlers and carpooled to work. A war in the Persian Gulf between Iraq and Iran compelled both member countries of OPEC to increase their production to meet the hefty cost of destruction. Furthermore, the discoveries of huge oil reserves in the North Sea basin presented OPEC with real competition in the world market. The balance of supply and demand finally worked—to the astonishment of all observers—and the price per barrel was split in half. The mightiest of all cartels is now divided and unable to unify its members.

Another big speculative bubble that burst in the past few years was the speculative fever of gold. After the United States abandoned the gold standard in 1971, the price of that precious metal, which had been floated at $35 per troy ounce, started to move upward. During the 1970s, gold prices kept rising to ever-higher levels. The roaring inflation that plagued the decade fueled the final speculative binge, which carried gold's

price to $800 per troy ounce—over 20 times its original float-
ing price—in just nine years. At its peak, experts, citing runaway inflation, predicted that gold would soar above the
$1,000 mark. Yet the trend started, heightened, and then had a
traumatic ending. Unless another wave of hyperinflation hits
the economy again, the price of gold may not rise for many
years to come to its all-time high reached in 1980.

One final example to illustrate the traumatic ending of
speculative bubbles—no matter who is sponsoring them—is
the price of silver, which came under heavy speculation
fueled by the appetite of some great tycoons. In the late seventies, the price of silver, which is also an important industrial
metal, rose from a little under $5 to over $50 per ounce. Speculators were faced with a market that appreciated more than
ten times within a few months. In less than a month, silver
prices experienced a straight-line decline. After an initial
plummet below $10 per ounce, the price gradually made its
way back to its original price; since then it has been meander-
ing around those levels.

TALES OF SHAKEOUT CITY

Similarly today, the housing boom in California and
Texas has reached the point of no return—for what could be a
long time ahead. The speculative bubble ended, as did all
other previous speculative bubbles.

In Texas, the fastest-growing state in the nation during
the seventies, bankruptcies have been rising and real estate
values have been plummeting. Oil prices are down, and red
ink is everywhere. The crisis took its toll on both banks and
individuals. Several banks that extended loans to oil companies and to individuals who bought real estate suffered and
continue to suffer loan losses and defaults.

In the agricultural sector, farmers incurred their largest
losses since the Great Depression. Banks that had extended
loans to farmers have failed with record numbers not seen
since the agricultural depression of the early twenties. Even

now, no relief seems to be in sight, and the process of debt liquidation is continuing.

Single-family housing in the Northeast has stopped advancing in price since mid-1986. When such a condition prevails, it usually indicates that supply and demand are in equilibrium. This is known among real estate professionals as "a buyers' market," in which it is easier to buy than to sell at desired prices. This stage tends to develop ahead of major trend reversals.

The great office buildings' boom has already entered a period of adjustment and the vacancy rate in major cities has been rising. Moreover, many large corporations have sold their headquarters in prestigious business locations and corporations have moved some of their operations to the suburbs. This, too, has accentuated the situation of overcapacity that exists in the office building sector.

The debt accumulated in this sector is large, and it will take several years until this liquidation process is complete. According to a study by Arthur Andersen & Co. and the Massachusetts Institute of Technology, only 897 million square feet of the 1.3 billion square feet built between 1975 and 1985 were needed. This overcapacity, especially in the wake of a business slowdown, will take a number of years to resolve. Lenders have already become more cautious and have cut back on financing new projects.

Finally, the stock market crash of 1987 has raised further doubts and exercised further pressure on the future of real estate nationwide, especially in the Northeast. While the real estate slowdown has already materialized in the West Coast and has precipitated a depression in Texas and most of the agricultural states, it has lagged behind in the Northeast. Not only were those states slow in catching up with the boom when it first started, but they also resisted the initial decline of real estate prices in other parts of the nation.

New York City is the home of banking and finance. The stock market boom has helped to delay price deflation, which is already taking its toll on other big cities. Before the stock market crash of 1987, business was great, with the historic boom in financial markets. The melting of values in the securities market represents the first genuine threat to the real estate boom in the Big Apple. Jobs in the financial community may continue to be at risk. The economy of New York City may undergo a period of adjustment similar in magnitude to that which Texas underwent in the wake of the oil price decline.

REASONS FOR THE SLOWDOWN

The unrelenting advance in the prices of houses may have reached its extreme highs for the next ten years and possibly for the early part of the next century. Several factors have been in the making during the 1980s that do not bode well for the future of real estate.

During the first half of the 1980s, household debt rose to its highest level in this century. The ratio of debt to personal income reached a whopping 17 percent. And this debt accumulation has taken place in an environment of declining unemployment and booming stock and bond markets. Cutbacks in the financial services sector may have begun and could continue in earnest for the next few years. At the first shadow of rising unemployment, the debt liquidation process may begin. Households that have extended beyond their means could have difficulty in meeting their mortgage payments and the ugly face of default may appear. Foreclosures are likely to take their toll on strapped budgets.

The supply of homes in the marketplace is expected to exceed demand, at which point prices can naturally begin to decline. The initial stage of the decline is likely to be contained, as new buyers will perceive declining house prices as bargains. However, as those residual prospective buyers disappear, prices may then continue on their downward course. The second wave of price declines, accompanied by further layoffs, could impose further pressures on family finances; more foreclosures may follow. The longer that process lasts, the lower prices could decline.

The high level of household debt is not the only reason for the expected slowdown in real estate prices. Savings rates are also at their lowest level for the past three decades. This means that the reserves that families would normally tap during hard times have shrunk. It is true, on the other hand, that families with two wage-earners may be able to absorb the financial loss of unemployment. Nevertheless, they may not have much room to maneuver.

In addition to the above factors, the crash in securities prices eliminated a good deal of household liquidity. During the stock market advance, many individuals and families borrowed against their home equities to invest in the stock market. With these losses incurred in equities, families and individuals have to meet loans from their earned income alone. Again, the prospect of a mild recession or a modest rise in unemployment could exert some financial pressure on their capacity to meet their debts. If the recession ahead happens to be severe, the decline in real estate prices may be substantial.

Also, the big rush of the baby boomers to the residential end of the real estate market appears to have peaked. The growth of the labor force has also gone past its peak, given the demographic statistics available today. Those two factors could put an end to the last demand for houses.

Finally, we have recently noticed a phenomenon that can only take place at the climax of a speculative boom. "No money down" programs have been broadcast all over the country. Smart tycoons who claim to have made fortunes in real estate have been preaching the inner secrets of their success to the average person. Magazines have been dedicated to detailing the secret ways that make master financiers acquire wealth in real estate. They encouraged people to enroll in real estate courses that can make them millionaires overnight— no matter who they are or what they know. Indeed, if this is not the sign of the end of the boom, we wonder what is.

FUTURE WAVES

A slowdown in real estate activities could have a serious impact on the economic outlook for the next few years. The inflation of the 1970s led people and the administrators to expect it to resurge at any time. We would like to caution those who are worried about a resurgence of inflation that they are fighting the wrong war and focusing their attention on the wrong issue. We think that the future has a surprise for families and individuals who still have great expectations for their investments in real assets. A decline in real estate activities is deflationary by nature, as it causes the price of properties to falter. And the forces of declining prices are greater than those of inflation.

The major factors that led to the substantial appreciation in real estate values were demographic in nature. They were exaggerated by runaway inflation, which coincided with them. Now, both the residential and business sectors of the housing market are suffering from excess inventory and overcapacity. The debt accumulated in that sector of the economy, which was brought about by years of economic expansion, may have to go through a liquidation process.

This expected slowdown in the real estate market could affect realtors, households, banks, and other financial institutions to a varying degree. It may lead to a general slowdown in business. In fact, the stock market may have already arrived at that conclusion. Banks, in particular, are faced with more than just the extended real estate sector. An above-average slowdown in the housing market could have a serious impact on their profitability. The best that the Federal Reserve Board (FED) and Washington can do at this stage is to recognize the effect of this important sector on the overall economic performance and factor it into their policies. Any restrictive policy could worsen the outcome and precipitate an above-average business contraction.

However, for households that are not extended and that do not have a large debt outstanding, things should be normal. Cycles of boom and bust in the real estate sector are not new to our economy. Weathering of the expected slowdown is likely to be followed by another rebound in real estate values, once we are ready for the next expansion in business activities.

THE OPTIMIST SPEAKS

We have already presented the factors behind the phenomenal boom in real estate. We also cited some of the factors that could affect its future prospects in relation to the overall business environment. The point we are trying to make is that a great deal of uncertainty surrounds this vital sector of the economy.

In our study of the factors influencing the future of real estate, we are not predicting a bust. Many households today have two paychecks that could meet mortgage payments. The majority of houses are bought to host members of the family. Through good times or bad times, people are proud of owning their own houses. In any case, owning is much better than wasting money on rent. Eventually, homeowners end up with equity when they decide to sell their homes.

Real estate investments are superb for the long term. However, in the short term, the prices of houses fluctuate depending upon supply and demand. In the past, business has always been able to recover from periods of slowdown. In the future, business will still come back. The fact that prices may soften in the immediate future should not be alarming. The cycle simply got extended and may have to undergo an adjustment. However, this does not spell doom to real estate investors. For some, as a matter of fact, it may be just the opportunity that they have been waiting for.

There is room for optimism in the future. One positive development that could put the lid on the decline of real estate in America is the weak dollar. The precipitous decline of our currency in the foreign exchange market has created bargains for foreigners. Several Japanese firms and wealthy foreign individuals have been buying prime real estate properties. In real terms, despite the price appreciation of the eighties, real estate is cheap in the United States when taking into consideration the dollar decline. Even if the value of the dollar stabilizes in comparison to other currencies, it should still render real estate prices cheap for foreign investors.

This does not imply that every house may not suffer some decline in its price. However, prices in metropolitan areas may not decline that much. Moreover, prices should rebound at the first sign of revival in business activities.

THE BEST INVESTMENT IN THE NEXT CENTURY

The baby boomers played a major role in the real estate boom of the seventies and eighties. In the next few years, some residual buying demand may be left; otherwise, the housing market will be, at best, flat. During the 1990s, real estate activities may continue to be subdued. As demand moderates, prices could stabilize. For the average investor, it will not be easy to make a killing.

In the longer term, the future may hold a once-in-a-lifetime opportunity for patient money. The baby boomers were born between 1945 and 1960. In the United States, they constitute a large percentage of the population. In the early part of the next century, they will be retiring, when a large number of them are expected to migrate to states in which the weather is warmer. The southern states may have to accommodate a substantial number of retirees. Demand in those states could exceed supply. Prices of real estate could appreciate significantly in the South. In the early part of the twenty-first century, Florida, long known as a retirement haven, could present the best investment opportunity. The price of land, houses, and even rentals could soar. Prices in the South may start to adjust as early as the mid-nineties for that expected rise in value. Acceleration of this advance could start in earnest at the onset of the next century. For those who can afford patience, real estate may present the best investment of their lifetime.

❑ 6

The Industrial Samurai

The Rise of Japan Inc.

"Time is a Master Worker that heals the wounds of temporary defeat, and equalizes the inequalities and rights the wrongs of the world. There is nothing 'Impossible' with time!"

Napoleon Hill

A major reason behind our deteriorating competitiveness, both domestically and abroad, is the rise of Japan as a serious industrial contender. Japanese products have flooded the world market. The industrial samurai has challenged the dominance of American multinationals in the global arena. His aggressive and unrelenting invasion precipitated the downfall of U.S. manufacturing and inflicted a severe imbalance in our international trade. To get back on track and to regain our leadership in the world market, we have no alternative but to learn from our mistakes.

How did Japan grow from a fragile assembly-line manufacturer to an economic superpower? What helped it to achieve its legendary success? What are the secrets behind its high productivity? What can we learn from the Japanese experience? Can their growth continue forever, or are we witnessing the sunset of the industrial samurai?

CAUGHT OFF GUARD

Japan came out of World War II defeated. The bitterness of this decisive loss could have held it back for years. Yet with great resolve and perseverance, Japan's young generation overcame its shame and had great hopes.

Thirty years later, Japan became the twentieth-century legend that the world admires. Manufacturing started as an assembly-line operation, imitating products of other countries. Japanese companies aimed at the world as their prospective market and slowly but surely learned the business of international trade. They became known for quality and flooded their targeted markets with cheap products.

Japanese executives toured Europe and had their eyes on the consumer market. They watched the Swiss building watches, took some pictures of foreign manufacturing facilities, and went back home to duplicate them. Before anyone knew it, Japan had monopolized the watch business. It put a dramatic end to Swiss dominance of the watch market. Next, Japanese firms aimed at the camera market and flooded the globe with cameras of better quality and cheaper prices. They eliminated the competition; brand-name camera manufacturers kept disappearing one after another. Shortly after, they established dominance in the consumer electronic market. They flooded the world with televisions, radios, tape recorders, and video equipment. They transistorized the business and created a market for the Walkman.

In the late seventies, helped by the energy crisis, they launched their attack on the U.S. automobile industry. They dared to challenge General Motors, Ford, and Chrysler. The automakers suffered their worst setback since the depression and were quick to seek government protection. Japanese companies excelled in large-scale integration and threatened U.S. presence in the fastest-growing industry in the world. They captured over 60 percent of market share in the semiconductor industry. Their technology became vital to the missiles and fighters that defend the West. In the eighties, Japan took aim at financial markets and established the top brokers in the business.

It took a great deal of determination, perseverance, and sense of direction for a young generation of a defeated nation to overcome adversity and to soar in the global market. Japan is running a trade surplus with just about every major economy in the world. Its superiority is verifiable in all business statistics. The legendary achievement of Japanese companies has introduced into the dictionary a large number of new names such as Mitsubishi, Honda, Seiko, Toyota, Mitsui, Namura, and Toshiba.

THE MAKEUP OF A LEGEND

Japan's success story in the world market is the envy of all nations. In the process of competing with Japanese firms, several industries suffered severe dislocations in their domestic markets.

Several factors contributed to the phenomenal growth of Japan. Since the beginning, the Japanese had a well-thought-out master plan that integrated their business and social resources and targeted them toward achieving their ambitious goals. In addition, Japanese corporations effectively used high leverage during the early stages of their industrial development. Management style also had its share in nurturing growth. The paternalistic relationship between business and labor contributed to productivity and efficiency.

Government support of long-term goals further helped Japanese firms to execute their plans. The government helped to coordinate their activities in a harmonious business symphony. Cultural factors were also key in creating an environment that led to the ultimate triumph. Finally, the changing marketplace and a stroke of blind luck helped Japan to capture a decent share of the venerable automobile market in America. A quick review of these factors should be instrumental in helping us to formulate our own future plans.

THE MASTER PLAN

The Japanese style of dominating the world market was based on gaining market share. They initially implemented that strategy through price mechanisms. Those were the days of the early 1960s, when Japanese products were considered low-tech junk. During this early stage, Japan had an important competitive advantage: cheap labor. However, U.S. multinationals were on solid ground, and "Made in America" was the mark of quality and competitiveness. The Japanese's low-pricing tactics had a mixed success at the beginning.

The second phase of the master plan combined quality with the low-price advantage. That's when Juran's role in modern industrial Japan came in. J. M. Juran, a Roumanian immigrant and founder of the Juran Institute Inc. in Wilton, Connecticut, taught the Japanese the virtue of upgrading the quality of their management and production. He was awarded Japan's highest honor for foreigners in recognition of his consultations on quality achievement. Quality management in Japan became a way of life, and its power began to work in the late sixties and early seventies.

The true break for Japan came in the wake of the first oil shock. The price of gasoline rose. Energy conservation and fuel efficiency ranked among the most desired features by the consumers in the United States. The auto industry was caught off guard. The three giant auto manufacturers were not in a position to compete: General Motors and Ford were still banking on the high profit margin of big cars, and Chrysler was a ghost of a company, suffering from severe financial problems. Japanese companies used their superiority in manufacturing small and midsized cars to gain ground in the wide-open American market.

That marked the beginning of good times for Japanese products. The fad began, and "buy Japanese" gained momentum. The consumer's perception of their quality accelerated their industrial penetration of the U.S. market. This explosion of Japanese exports afforded them the wealth that helped them to develop further their industrial base.

As their penetration of the world market gained momentum, the sales volume of their competitors, predominantly American companies, declined. This loss of sales worldwide took away from U.S. manufacturers badly needed cash flow. Productivity suffered with this loss of market share. Many American manufacturers were suddenly unable to compete on a worldwide scale and suffered huge losses. This lost cash flow ended up in the pockets of Japanese producers who, in turn, plowed it back into their businesses. It allowed them to gain economies of scale and to further enhance their market share.

As their products gained brand recognition and became associated with quality in the minds of consumers, the third phase of their master plan was implemented. Once in control, the Japanese started to raise the prices of their products to boost profit margins.

To summarize, the Japanese master plan was to sacrifice profit margins at the early stages of market penetration. This allowed them to acquire a substantial market share in targeted industries. In most cases, their competitors were unable to compete with their aggressive pricing strategy and experienced difficulties in operating at a profit. The market was then flooded with products at discount prices, and the number of competitors was reduced as some decided to abandon such markets. The Japanese machine then gradually raised its prices to recapture all the profits that were sacrificed at the beginning. During this process, economies of scale were realized. Moreover, once total monopoly of an industry was realized, the cumulative technological and market experience became Japanese.

THE GENIUS OF LEVERAGE

Corporate management in Japan opted for growth which was achieved at the expense of profits, at least until full market penetration was achieved. Shareholders in Japan accepted to foresake short-term financial rewards to accommodate management goals.

Aggressive financial strategies were pursued to attain exceptional growth. Japanese companies used special banking relationships to borrow funds to finance their investment needs. Their high-growth targets necessitated aggressive debt financing. During the seventies, the debt to equity ratio of the average Japanese manufacturer exceeded 2:1. By American standards, those levels of debt were not considered prudent. Banks would not approve of them, shareholders would reject them, and analysts would scream about them.

Once the market share strategy succeeded and prices were raised, profit margins increased and debt was paid off. Moreover, as growth was achieved, the debt to equity ratio declined. Japanese companies were able to satisfy their financial needs from internally generated profits. Today, Japanese companies are not as leveraged as they used to be.

Here again, the financial structure of the Japanese firms served the ambitious growth objectives of the master plan. In the final analysis, the strategy worked. While profits were sacrificed during the 1960s, their gained competitiveness on a global scale allowed Japanese companies to expand their businesses and to establish monopolies in several industries. This fostered further breakthroughs in new manufacturing methods and enabled them to gain economies of scale and pay off their debts. Shareholders were handsomely compensated by hefty returns on equity, averaging 20 percent during the 1970s.

AT THE EXPENSE OF A WHOLE GENERATION

Japan has many natural obstacles to internal development. Due to its mountainous terrain, only 20 percent of the land is usable. Half of this is dedicated to the farming industry. Highways are congested. Cities, which are overpopulated, are built on less than 2 percent of the land.

The supereconomy of Japan was built at the expense of the generation that witnessed in great shame its bitter defeat in World War II. The Japanese people sacrificed their individuality and worked hard as members of their companies, where they were promised lifetime job security.

During the early days of Japan's industrialization, Japanese consumers saved as much as they could even though they paid the highest price for food in the world. They skipped vacations and endured a severe housing shortage.

They saved and saved and saved for that rainy day that never came. The savings rate in Japan has been no less than phenomenal. In 1965, it was 17.2 percent; in 1970, it rose to 20.3 percent; in 1973, it jumped to 22.5 percent. Amid the oil crisis in 1974, it reached an unbelievable 24.3 percent. Between 1975 and 1980, it consistently hovered between 20 percent and 23 percent. In 1985, it was still running high at 22.5 percent. No wonder that the Japanese financial institutions are now awash with cash and challenging the mighty U.S. banks.

This pattern of strong competition, which has characterized the Japanese trading style, has also been the rule in the domestic economy. Companies in the same industry suffer from severe internal competition. Only the cream of the crop stands a chance to rise to international status. The benefits of Japan's success have not been shared equally by all sectors. Most of the country's savings were channeled into manufacturing.

However, change is now upon Japan. It has a population older than that of any Western nation. In the year 2000, the elderly will constitute about 20 percent of the population—far above that of any other industrial country. The gray-haired retirees may have to choose to live in a place outside of Japan because of soaring prices of land and real estate.

Moreover, Japanese companies have recently announced that they are shifting from their paternalistic style of employment. The strength of the yen has imposed strains on the employer-employee relationship. Layoffs have been rising, which is shattering a long-standing tradition of job security that Japan once bragged about.

The new generation of Japanese are different from their parents. They put family ahead of career. While their parents remained loyal to their companies, they maintain an independent and individualistic attitude. They are attracted by fads and fashions and take affluence for granted. Unlike their parents, they do not view work as virtuous but as unavoidable. They base their decisions on feelings, rather than on morals as their parents have done. This young generation of Japan represents another side of the samurai. They are highly educated, open to international influence, and less keen on competition. The "me generation" has finally found its way to Japan.

SUCCESS ... THE JAPANESE WAY

Experts disagree on the reasons behind Japan's stunning achievement in the global industrial arena. At first, Japan was not considered a serious competitor; its products were perceived as cheap imitations of those manufactured by American and European multinationals.

Then opinion shifted in favor of their excellent automation facilities and their modern factory machines. Some who visited Japanese manufacturing facilities praised their cleanliness, their efficient handling of inventory controls, their quality circles, their superior production monitoring, and their efficient scheduling of both manufacturing and preventive maintenance. Some observers praised the dedication of their employees to perfection and quality and their lower absenteeism, hard work, corporate loyalty, and time consciousness. We also heard about Japanese management formulating long-term plans, maintaining a paternalistic relationship with employees, relying more on engineers and technically skilled workers, efficiently using their unique capital structure, and maintaining a special relationship with their bankers and the government, which provides unlimited support.

A FINANCIAL GOLIATH

In the mid-1980s, financial institutions in Japan dominated the list of the largest banks and brokers in the world
because Japanese exports brought home a large surplus and
swelled savings. Using the same techniques of competition
that proved successful in manufacturing, banks have been
repackaging loans at much lower interest. Since Japanese
savings accounts are paid much lower interest rates than in
the United States, Japanese financial institutions have even
more resources and are able to extend loans to American
corporations below the best rates that they can get from the
large U.S. banks.

Here again, the strategy is to establish a respectable market
share position at the expense of profits. The Japanese produce
a cheaper copy of American banks' products and make it
difficult for them to compete. At the brokerage end, they have
underwritten securities and bonds at lower commissions for
major corporate clients as well as state and local governments.
They have been major buyers of U.S. Treasury bonds, and they
are claimed to be financing the ballooning U.S. government
deficit. In addition, they have extended loans to corporations
involved in leveraged buyouts and have formed syndicates
with American and European financial lending institutions.
The Japanese strategy in banking and brokerage has allowed
them to gain a respectable market share around the globe.

WHEN ADMIRATION TURNS TO ANGER

The legend of the sweeping success of the industrial
samurai was greeted with admiration during the seventies. It
had all the mystique of a defeated nation that was able to circumvent all adversities and prevail. It attracted sympathy for
a country that rose from the ashes of destruction to earn its
place as an international superstar. Indeed, we salute Japan for

doing what no other nation has done in such a short period of time.

But it has reached a point at which the insistence of the samurai on dominating and monopolizing international markets has inflicted economic pain on other nations. Japan is now an economic superpower and the largest creditor nation in the world. In 1987, the bilateral trade deficit between the United States and Japan reached a little over $60 billion, which is politically and economically unsustainable.

Moreover, American multinationals remain locked out of the Japanese market. U.S. construction companies were prohibited from bidding on the Kansai Airport, which is considered one of the largest construction projects in the world. They were also prevented from bidding on the construction of Tokyo Bay Bridge. In 1986, while Japanese construction firms did $2.3 billion worth of business in the United States, American companies did only a scant $1.4 million in Japan. The Japanese claimed that American firms failed to obtain general construction licenses.

In 1986, the United States exported only 2,345 cars to Japan, while Japan exported a whopping 2.3 million cars to the United States. Globally, Japan exported 4.5 million cars and imported only 68,000 cars, including Mercedes, BMW, Volvo, and other foreign cars. The Japanese claim that U.S. firms have not made any effort to develop their market in Japan. They also claim that American companies do not manufacture a right-side steering-wheel car.

Japanese farmers are totally protected. The price of rice in Japan is seven times the world market price. In more general terms, farm products cost two to seven times more in Japan than in the rest of the world. Whenever the Japanese are asked to open their markets, their leaders are quick to diffuse the issue with warm words and occasional token concessions.

Western countries have been calling on Japan to assume greater responsibility in maintaining the world economy. The global economy has been sluggish during most of the 1980s, and Third World countries have been struggling to increase their share of exports to pay their huge debts. Cash-rich

Japanese banks have been called upon to increase their lending to debt-ridden Third World countries and to recycle their huge surpluses to less developed countries (LDCs). In addition, the Japanese government was urged to drop its trade barriers to Third World products. LDCs are in dire need of exporting their commodities if they are ever to meet their hefty obligations. In 1986, the United States imported over 60 percent of total LDC exports, Europe imported 22 percent, but Japan imported a slim 8 percent.

Japan cannot escape its responsibility as one of the most powerful nations in the West. Japan is an economic superpower, and its Western partners have been rightfully urging it to recycle the proceeds from its mammoth trade surplus back into the world economy and to step up aid to developing countries. Loans should be made available to more countries. Allocations of grants should be expanded, and technical assistance should also be improved.

TENSION ACROSS THE PACIFIC

Japan is not a country endowed with abundant natural resources. It has a constant fear of being unable to meet its food and energy needs unless it maintains an export base to support its domestic demands.

Prior to World War II, Japan used to compensate for its lack of resources by direct aggressive military action. Earlier this century, Japan invaded its neighbors, including Russia and China. After World War II, the Japanese put on a three-piece suit and emerged as the industrial samurai.

Since World War II, Japan has been able to separate its political and military objectives from its economic goals. Since Japan's defense budget does not exceed 1 percent of its GNP, it has been able to maximize its growth by concentrating on building an export-oriented economy. Despite the fact that Japan imports 55 percent of its oil needs from the Persian Gulf, Japanese vessels are absent from the region. Western nations are now questioning whether Japan can remain a great economic power without assuming parallel responsibilities in political affairs. Japan replies that their constitution prohibits them from building a large army or from deploying existing forces out of its immediate surroundings.

Japan is one of America's best allies. We have a vested political and economic interest in its status as an important economic power in the Far East. However, it has now reached the point at which Japan's greed has caused pain to Western economies. During the 1980s, in a shrinking global economy, Japan has been amassing the largest trade surplus of all industrial nations. It has pushed businesses into the red and dislocated several industrial sectors in America and Europe.

Voices in Washington and around the world have been asking government to take decisive action to protect domestic markets from Japanese competition. Japan has been accused of unjustifiable and unreasonable trade practices. It has been blamed for substantial injury to domestic industries. While Japan is rampaging the world with its products, it has kept its market closed and has retarded the development of its own domestic market.

In the 1980s, Japan may have seen its best days under the sun. With the recent strength of the yen, internal dislocations and recessionary pressures are mounting. Restructuring of its economy has to occur in the coming decade, and a severe slowdown in its export revenues may eventually balance its trade position with that of the rest of the world. With business and political tensions mounting, Japan may not have much room in which to maneuver in coming years.

ENDAKA ... THE PERILS OF THE MIGHTY YEN

It seemed as if nothing could stop Japan from assaulting the world's markets. It became a legend in the lexicon of industrial economics. It seemed that the only way to slow down the unstoppable Japanese was protectionism. Having gone through the perils of the "beggar thy neighbor" era, another bold step had to be initiated, which was admitting that the U.S. dollar was overvalued.

Before the resultant shock to the yen, Japanese companies were increasing their manufacturing base abroad to sidestep trade barriers and to overcome protectionist sentiment against them. However, the rise of the yen probably inflicted more pain in Japan than the experts would have imagined. The yen's meteoric rise has two effects on Japan's industrial infrastructure and its domestic economy.

The impact of *endaka* was to shift Japanese production overseas. Japan exported its own manufacturing companies and shipped its factories abroad. Staying in their homeland was very devastating for its exports, which almost instantly became overpriced. This has undoubtedly damaged their competitive edge.

Manufacturing outside Japan deprives Japanese firms of access to parts manufacturers, which in their country helps avoid stacking of inventory. This Japanese innovation, known as "just-in-time," is one of the points of strength in their manufacturing structure. Another drawback of manufacturing outside Japan is the loss of employees' loyalty in foreign lands.

Over the past decade, Japan lost its price competitiveness as the wages of its labor force caught up with those of other industrial nations. It began to feel the pinch of enjoying a higher standard of living and the cost that accompanies it. For a long time, the Japanese have been proud of their paternalistic employment record, which in fact they may have copied from IBM. Now the bonds between employer and employee have weakened. With the severe adjustment that their economy is going through, lifetime employment has been denied; many Japanese workers may feel that they have been left behind and that the system has reneged on its promises.

Direct foreign investment has surged and is expected to continue to rise for a long time. Japan's direct investment overseas should catch up with that of the United States and the United Kingdom. Over one-third of its investments are in America. And why not? The Japanese are happy to move closer to their best allies and the most lucrative market in the world. According to Lloyds' statistics, more than 70 percent of Japan's exports are machinery and automobiles, with a large percentage of that from the U.S. market.

On the positive side, Japanese offshore manufacturing allows them to move closer to their prospective markets and hence save on transportation and distribution costs. Moreover, overseas investment helps to circumvent trade friction, defuse trade barriers, spur local economies, and provide jobs in countries where they are manufacturing.

The Japanese government has been, as usual, assisting offshore manufacturing by organizing orientation seminars on overseas investments, providing consultation services, and issuing survey information. The government has also been generous with financing to ease the initial burden.

INTERLOCKING DESTINIES

The industrial samurai has now shifted course. He did little to open his own market and to abide by the rules of free trade. Instead, he is pouring his huge balance of trade surpluses into and moving his industrial base to America. His plan is now to reach deep into the heartland of the most highly developed market in the world to weather the wave of mounting protectionism and to interlock his economic fortune with that of the leader of the West.

Japanese investments have found a home in major cities across the land. They have been buying premium real estate in Manhattan, Chicago, Los Angeles, and other places. Awash with cash from exports, Japanese banks and brokerage houses have also decisively moved into U.S. financial markets. They have provided billions of dollars to states, cities, businesses, and universities. Their capital is made available to companies in ailing industries, which American banks would consider out of the realm of prudence. More important, they are backing up their aggressive industrial expansion in North America.

Japan's investment in North America is growing in leaps and bounds. It has tripled from 1980 to 1985. According to Japan's Ministry of International Trade and Industry, those investments are expected to grow at better than 14 percent annually by the end of this century. Hundreds of companies have set up manufacturing facilities in North America. Some Japanese companies have even bought large stakes in American firms. Nippon Kokan acquired a 50 percent stake in National Steel Corp. Nishin Steel holds 66 percent of Wheeling Pittsburgh Steel Corporation. Kawasaki Steel owns half of California Steel Corporation. A consortium of three Japanese companies bought two plants from Firestone Tire & Rubber. Honda, Nissan, and Toyota established plants in Kentucky, Tennessee, and Ohio.

Not only are they adding problems to the eroding share of American companies in the vital automobile market, but they are competing with auto parts manufacturers in the domestic market. With the excuse of preservation of quality, Japanese car makers import their parts from Japan. *In short, Japanese firms are proceeding with their penetration of the U.S. auto markets and the industries that are related to it.*

The industrial samurai's initiatives have been met with enthusiasm by city, state, and local officials. Japanese companies have been given tax breaks and special privileges. Some state officials have embraced the U.S.-Japanese companies as saviors of ailing industries. They figure that the legendary Japanese know-how and abundant capital will revive local economies and create wealth.

Japan's announced motivation is to stop the migration of jobs from the United States and to create work for the unemployed. It is a show of faith, they contend, to cooperate with American firms to increase the effectiveness of our production. They claim that they are bringing their distinctive management and quality methods of manufacturing to help balance the trade deficit. Their unrevealed intentions, however, are to counteract the perilous consequences of the soaring yen and its devastating effect on their past glory.

Japan does not have the cheap labor that once helped it to compete. Protectionist sentiment has compelled Washington to reevaluate its trade relationship with Japan and to formulate a strategy to stop the bleeding of American business. Meanwhile, Japanese corporations have moved promptly to establish a manufacturing base in the United States before the gates of free trade between the two nations are closed.

PATRIOTISM OF A SECOND-CLASS CITIZEN

Japan's inroads into manufacturing at the domestic level raise serious questions. The Japanese claim that their businesses are creating jobs in depressed areas and are helping to revive aging industries. They are taking a step toward reducing the U.S. trade deficit and are helping us increase our exports to Japan and other parts of the world. Even if this is true, severe repercussions could result from such a trend.

First of all, we should notice that the Japanese style in finance and banking is not different from that used previously in manufacturing: abundance at a cheap price. Banks and brokers have been offering sizable funds at very competitive interest rates. Where U.S. banks consider it imprudent to lend, the Japanese financier has been generous despite the risks. Because of their growing capital base from exports, they have aggressively pursued this risky strategy to gain market presence. Also, they enjoy low capital requirements since they are not members of the Federal Reserve system. While U.S. banks have to maintain reserves mandated by the FED, Japanese financial institutions do not have to abide by these rules, they can *afford* to lend at cheaper rates.

Unfortunately, the process of selective Japanese acquisition of American firms could lead to loss of control over strategic decisions at the top. It could also mean that acquired corporations would have to serve long-term goals that may not necessarily agree with our national interests.

Manufacturing in the continental United States may intensify management-union friction for many local manufacturers. In their efforts to compete at cheaper prices, American companies may not be able to honor their unions' demands. This has already presented a serious threat to automakers, tire and rubber producers, machinery manufacturers, auto parts companies, and—most important—Silicon Valley, where, as a nation, we have a vested interest. Does Japanese involvement in the domestic economy stimulate manufacturing or add to the industrial dislocation that their earlier aggressive strategies led to?

We question the patriotism of the second-class citizen and wonder if it could lead to any improvement in the industrial sector in the long term. The Japanese are likely to insist on having the upper hand in final decisions. We doubt that the objectives of the Japanese will serve our purposes and economic goals. Moreover, Japanese investments could wipe out a good deal of the engineering and technical work force that translates raw technology into finished products.

AND NOW ... THE DISINCORPORATION OF JAPAN INC.?

Early in 1987, the Keizai Koho Center, Japan's Institute for Social and Economic Affairs, published a report entitled "Japan's Strong Yen Crisis—The Shock Spreads." This report includes six articles published in *The Japan Times* about the severe damage that the strong yen is inflicting on the economy.

First, the Japanese shipbuilding industry is sinking fast. The industry has survived the disasters of the oil shocks of the seventies, but the yen shock is pushing it quickly into a state of collapse. The *endaka-fukyo*, the recession caused by the strong yen, has precipitated a decline in orders received by Japanese companies by 40 percent in 1986 compared with the previous year. This was one-third of the level recorded in 1983.

The steel industry, too, is suffering a hemorrhage because of the steep rise of the yen and intense competition from South Korea. Furnaces were extinguished as demand for steel cooled off. Nippon Steel Corp., the largest steel maker in Japan, led the way by laying off some 19,000 employees. The Labor Ministry estimated that there are more than 30,000 surplus workers in the industry.

And the list of casualties of the mighty yen is spreading all over the country of the industrial samurai. The textile industry, which has been struggling to survive, is in a severe slump. Many manufacturers are closing their factories and creating an unemployment problem of major proportions.

Indeed, the crisis is also hitting successful industries that helped the export might of Japan, such as automobile, toy, electronic appliance, and office equipment industries. The strength of the yen translates into more expensive Japanese products in the world market; several rounds of markups were initiated by automakers and other export-oriented manufacturers. The competitiveness of Japanese products is losing ground against restructuring American multinationals, which are regaining their trading edge. In addition, the progressive Far Asian industrial states—Korea, Taiwan, Singapore, and Hong Kong—are flooding the world with low-priced manufactured goods. A wave of subtle protectionism is adding to the troubles of the export business in Japan.

Ironically, offshore manufacturing is causing Japan Inc. to suffer from hollowing, the same disease it gave Western industrial nations. As more Japanese companies are shifting their production facilities to more competitive economies around the world, employers have no choice but to resort to layoffs. The jobless rate is soaring, as several companies are facing lower revenues. The Ministry of International Trade and Industry in Japan is predicting that some 800,000 jobs are at stake if the trend toward offshore manufacturing continues to surge at an annual rate of 20 percent. Moreover, in 1987, some 900,000 workers were classified as "jobless persons on payrolls."

This is seen as a dangerous trend, as it is putting an *end to the legend of corporate paternalism in Japan.* For the first time in many years, lifelong employment is being threatened, which is spreading mixed feelings among employees. Security is no longer taken for granted. Some observers predict social unrest and the end of the country's conservative party.

The strength of the yen has a serious deflationary effect on Japan's domestic economy. Corporate earnings have been on a sliding path. Japanese companies are forced to idle a good deal of their advanced manufacturing facilities. Their robots are gathering dust, which is lamented as a waste of one of their most valuable resources.

Coping with the strength of the Japanese yen is causing major restructuring in the Japanese economy. The problem of declining exports is affecting cities around the Japanese capital and threatening the business structure in localities that depend on exports for their mere survival. This transformation of the domestic economy is overwhelming and could challenge the Japanese economy for many years to come. Growth cannot continue unchecked forever, and Japan is no exception.

HOW MANY JAPANESE WON THE NOBEL PRIZE?

The legend of the industrial samurai will be remembered long after the great generation that built Japan. Despite this, Japan has been unable to prove that it can provide the world with new innovations. There is no doubt that the Japanese are probably the best imitators, but the Japanese have won only four Nobel Prizes in science, versus 142 for the United States. They built an economic superpower by assembling technologies discovered and developed in other nations.

They showed superiority to most other people of the world in self-organization and discipline. They should be proud of their perseverance and persistence in achieving their national goals. However, they have soared and become too greedy for their own good. They are not satisfied with part of the pie; they want it all. In the 1980s, when the world economy was, at best, sluggish, they gained ground in other markets while keeping their own closed. This alienated other nations, which adopted protectionist measures. The industrial samurai went for the kill—dislocating and ravaging markets around the world. And he did it indiscriminately—to industrialized and industrializing countries—until it became unsustainable.

The ugly face of protectionism around the world had to surface. Even after the Western economies grow again, the industrial samurai may have to remain in hibernation. Things may not return to what they were in Japan for a long time. And that is good news; America will reindustrialize and regain its long-lost manufacturing superiority.

With hindsight, Japan's emergence was a fascinating phenomenon that we were privileged to witness. A country without internal resources, with mountainous land, and with a low capital base takes on the world. A country without a base of innovation and with lower creativity was able to assemble its way to supremacy. A country that chased dreams and succeeded to create a unique position for itself in a competitive world.

Japan was also helped by timely oil shocks and by consumers around the world. *We the consumers* allowed Japan to prosper. Because we needed energy-efficient vehicles and we wanted to save, we bought Japanese. *We the consumers* forgot that the majority of the technological discoveries of the century took place in America. In search of cheaper energy, we bought their cars and then we found excuses to buy everything else Japanese. *We the consumers* never asked ourselves who would buy our products if we didn't. *We the consumers* helped the legend of Japan live and deprived corporate America of badly needed cash. And while *we the consumers* bought Japanese goods, their consumers did not buy ours. We encouraged our manufacturers to compete at cheaper levels and move overseas, only to leave many lost jobs behind. The result was a decade of hollowing of corporate America.

❏ 7

In Search of Identity

The Postindustrial Society

"The American's way through life lay along the road of self-reliance; only in extremity did he look to government or his neighbors for economic assistance."

Dr. Arthur F. Burns
Chairman of the Federal Reserve Board
1970–1978

Since the turn of the twentieth century, manufacturing has been the main source of economic growth in the United States. Our great scientific and technological discoveries have helped the manufacturing production process to reach the advanced level of efficiency that the world enjoys today. While the service sector has expanded substantially over the years, its role in the economy has been limited to fulfilling a complementary function of secondary, yet vital importance to manufacturing.

Blessed with a vast land, a skilled labor force, abundant natural resources, access to capital, innovative management, and a solid institutional structure, the United States emerged after World War I as the leader of Western civilization. Despite the setback of the Great Depression, the industrial revolution of the decades that followed contributed to a high standard of living. By the late 1960s, the United States' Gross National Product (GNP) approximated 40 percent of the world's output.

However, as early as the mid–1960s, productivity began to decline. Then, in the 1970s, many constraints were imposed on the economy. Several factors combined to exercise upward pressure on the overall price structure of goods and services. The roaring inflation of the decade inflicted serious dislocations in various sectors of the economy.

The entrance of the baby boom generation, with its modest education and job experience, precipitated a decline in productivity. And manufacturing started to lose ground to foreign countries. Stiff price competition from foreign products shifted consumers' preference to imports. The rise of Japan as a dominant power in international trade cost us billions of dollars of trade deficit. American-made products lost their appeal at the consumer level, as perception of their inferiority began to gain credence in the minds of consumers.

Since the late 1970s, the service sector began to grow in leaps and bounds. The decline of the industrial base has now reached an alarming stage, and the postindustrial era is here to stay. Manufacturing has been replaced by service.

What are the reasons behind the decline of productivity in America? How serious are the problems in manufacturing? Can we compete in the world market? Can we afford to delegate manufacturing to foreign entities? What are the long-term implications of this industrial decline? Can technology help at this stage? Can the service society fill the gap? What are our choices at this critical juncture of our economic history?

OF AILING GIANTS AND TIMES PAST

The victory of World War II vested us with the responsibility of rebuilding Europe and leading our allies toward economic prosperity. We opened our markets to other nations— both developed and developing. We felt we had a stake in bringing less developed countries (LDCs) up to speed. We strove to stop communism from spreading to other parts of the globe and checked its drive toward military superiority.

Major breakthroughs in science and technology allowed us to enjoy high productivity and a rising standard of living. "Made in America" was a big success overseas and a sign of quality and durability. Our dollar became the world reserve currency. Our markets grew and expanded—both domestically and abroad. In those days, American banks were mighty giants, far ahead of any foreign banks in both size and prestige.

In the 1960s, our economy grew at a faster rate. The gap between the United States and other Western nations began to widen. Meanwhile, the Japanese were still searching for their identity and formulating their plans to take over the international trade arena. Our prosperity gave way to management complacency. Corporate America did not suspect that serious contenders were about to crowd the scene. The "me generation" was growing and spreading its rebellious views of the world. The conflict in the Middle East destabilized that strategic and energy-rich region. We were taxed by the Vietnam War just when we had to turn our attention to the rising industrial samurai.

During this time, government became the fastest growing sector in America. Government intervention in all aspects of business mushroomed into all industrial sectors. And these policies encouraged consumption rather than savings. Businesses became entangled in red tape while foreign competitors were making inroads into our markets.

Therefore, the cost of running a business increased, and productivity suffered. What we thought to be a temporary statistical aberration in the mid-sixties was to intensify later, as the turbulent seventies began. Inflation was on the rise, and its evils were soon felt. As we entered the 1970s, we realized that the dollar was getting overvalued. Thus we adopted monetary policies designed to control inflation. Instead, they caused instability in our domestic economy. The resultant astronomical interest rates clobbered corporate finance and made the management of our institutions even more difficult.

With admiration, we watched our allies across the Pacific prosper. We witnessed the Japanese gain dominance in our domestic market. We closed our eyes to their protectionist attitude and abided by the rules of fair trade. We sacrificed our own markets on the altar of free enterprise. We silently observed our companies falling behind into noncompetitiveness. We shrugged our shoulders and advocated the free market. We thought we were in control and took our time in reassessing our options.

We welcomed the service society, thinking that it could afford us the high standard of living to which we had grown accustomed. We built more restaurants and ate more hamburgers while the steel industry was being ravaged by foreign competition. We reassured ourselves that we were simply living through a stage of transition in the postindustrial era. We felt secure that manufacturing could be delegated to other nations, and we only had to concern ourselves with the service sector.

Evidence of a manufacturing decline became overwhelming. Textiles, cotton fibers, leather, television, radio, consumer electronics, the auto industry, and others suffered severe blows to their markets' infrastructures. However, we managed to maintain growth in high tech until the early 1980s, when the industrial samurai claimed his final triumph. Sagging profitability, chronic unemployment, a staggering rise of imports, and an alarming level of corporate debt led to a sluggish economy and slow growth.

In the 1980s, disinflation became the new plague of the West. Economic growth was hard to achieve, and the pie of prosperity shrank. Budget and trade deficits grew in the Western nations. Ailing economies around the world suffered from sluggish business while Japan monopolized the global market. However, soon other rival competitors appeared in the international arena. The progressive arm of capitalism in the Far East—Taiwan, South Korea, Hong Kong, and Singapore—challenged the industrial samurai, and the price was right.

While the West continued to struggle with its eroding industrial base, the danger of deindustrialization became readily apparent. Governments around the world adopted nontariff barriers, and trade friction began to mount. Protectionism gained appeal among politicians, and the shadow of the "beggar thy neighbor" policies of the 1930s slowly reappeared, only to prove that history repeats itself.

THE DEINDUSTRIALIZATION OF CORPORATE AMERICA

It was Henry Ford who was responsible for the greatest manufacturing leap of this century to serve people's needs. It was Thomas Watson who turned a scales and clocks company into the legend of IBM. It was Alexander Graham Bell who allowed us to communicate thousands of miles apart. The list of those entrepreneurs who contributed to America's greatness is long. However, after years of innovation and a long track record of excellence, industrialization in America has fallen behind.

It is indeed a tragedy for the world to bypass the founder of modern capitalism in the global market. The car was invented and first produced in the United States, as were calculators, radios, recorders, televisions, transistors and chips, computers, and so on. Today, they are all made in Japan, Korea, Taiwan, and Europe. All these great inventions of the century, which were developed here in America, were handed over free to foreign assemblers. Total surrender became the norm rather than the exception. A mood of resignation and complacency replaced enthusiasm, leadership, and perseverance.

In the seventies and early eighties, corporations shied away from competing with the industrial samurai. Management was concerned with short-term profits and paid more attention to their figures on the ticker tape. Quarterly earnings and fancy analysts' reports distracted company executives from the long-term objectives of their institutions. They chose the easy ways out: manufacturing overseas or becoming the sales organizations to foreign suppliers. Instead of defending their markets and enduring the heat of competition, they sought refuge in marking time and looking to each other for bold answers. Management moved more and more toward reactionary crisis-handling rather than planning of long-term strategies. Protectionism, offshore manufacturing, international joint ventures, and automation loomed as possible answers to the manufacturing malaise. However, instead of addressing the source of our economic ailment, we pursued strategies that would make us look good in the next quarterly report. The "hollow corporation" became the new name for our once mighty multinationals.

And now we have to get back on track and revitalize our declining industrial base. We have to rebuild our manufacturing foundation. We have to take on the challenge of world globalization and reestablish ourselves as the unchallenged leader. Now is the time to regain our status as the world's largest creditor instead of the world's largest debtor. Now is the time to lead the world into the next century and bring back to our people the high standard of living they once had.

THE MYTH OF OUR DECLINING PRODUCTIVITY

Productivity is the key to competitiveness. Since the beginning of this century, gains in productivity have accounted for more than half of the growth of real GNP in the United States. Between 1916 and 1966, despite the Great Depression of the thirties, productivity grew on average at a healthy 2.2 percent. From 1944 to 1966, productivity grew at an astounding 3.2 percent. Since 1966, there has been a distinct decline in productivity, which grew at less than 2 percent. To uncover the reasons behind our economic problems, we have to study the causes of our faltering productivity.

There are several factors that contributed to the declining productivity of the past two decades. First there were changes in the labor force. The baby boomers were coming into the marketplace in large numbers with little experience and education. Also, women entered the job market and crowded the service sector.

These two factors have been changing as the labor force matured in experience and acquired higher education. So the decline of productivity at the end of the seventies was a transitory stage.

Moreover, in the seventies, existing production facilities did not expand fast enough to meet surging demand. Alarmed by inflation, the monetary authority tightened its reins severely, and interest rates soared. This, in turn, led to instability in the economy and deceleration in business growth.

Intense global competition from foreign products—especially those of the Japanese—has also impacted productivity. Since productivity is measured in terms of cost per man hour of work, severe price competition and the low sales volumes of domestic companies pushed up the price per unit produced, which translates into lower productivity. Dumping of foreign products into our markets influenced negatively the overall price structure of our manufacturing.

Increased government intervention prevented companies from effectively dealing with this declining competitiveness. Antitrust laws prohibited companies from consolidating their operations. This added indirectly to the cost per unit manufactured. In addition, pollution control requirements burdened industry with extra charges.

The substantial decline in the ratio of research and development (R&D) outlays to GNP deprived the economy of new technological sources of growth. Instead of concentrating on finding more efficient ways of production, companies concentrated on satisfying immediate demands.

In the seventies, complacency at the workers' level and the unions' extreme demands, without corresponding improvements in output, worsened productivity. Also, consumers went on a spending binge when they saw their nominal incomes increase. They apparently did not realize that after inflation they suffered a large loss in their purchasing power. Instead of striving to solve the declining standard of living, they consumed more and gave further ground to Japanese imports. The proliferation of negative social trends such as drug abuse, rising crime rates, and antiestablishment sentiments also contributed to the slide in productivity.

Most of those factors proved to be transitory. Today, inflation is subdued, and government intervention is decreased. The bulk of the cost of pollution control is behind us. The baby boomers are the new leaders of society, with more education and more experience. The strength of the yen is putting a dent in the supergrowth era of Japan; we are now beginning to resist their previously unchallenged invasion of our markets. The allocation of funds to R&D has been increasing since the mid-eighties, and automation and technological breakthroughs should continue to accelerate in the years ahead. Acceptance of automation has been gaining momentum and is enhancing office productivity. The learning curve of these new technical innovations has been rising steeply. Moreover, such technological advances will reduce unit costs and raise productivity.

THE ILLUSORY PARADISE OF THE SERVICE SOCIETY

Since the early seventies, economists have been discussing the evolution of the postindustrial society. The service sector, they contend, is taking over, whereas manufacturing is giving way. What exactly is the service society that everybody is talking about? What will happen to manufacturing? Can our world manage without it? Should we resign ourselves to offshore manufacturing and lose control of our production of goods? Will our national interests be jeopardized in the absence of manufacturing? Can we afford to let the steel industry, vital for defense, vanish?

The service society has been the backbone of all economic systems since the dawn of civilization. It has existed throughout history, long before the industrial revolution. At its basic definition, local hairdressers, army soldiers, bus drivers, cashiers, janitors, attendants, waiters, and waitresses are in the service sector. Those who look for a sophisticated way to describe it could include the accountant, the consultant, the banker, the nurse, the physician, the salesperson, and the pilot.

Manufacturing has been able, through the years, to create wealth and to contribute handsomely to our standard of living. In contrast, the service sector is characterized by low productivity and lower compensation. Also, the service sector is cyclical in nature, since companies as well as individuals tend to save on their service-related expenditures during recessions. The service sector depends on manufacturing for its own survival. Without manufacturing's production and creation of wealth, stagnant growth could be expected at best.

It is true, however, that the service industry grew during the 1970s. It created job opportunities that absorbed the flood of new entrants into the labor market. In fact, over 25 million such jobs were created from 1970 to 1986.

There are several factors behind the growth of the service sector in the past two decades. At the consumer end, the increased income of the two-paycheck family led to a leisure-oriented era, which used services out of convenience and growing affluence. The retail industry benefited from this increased wealth and expanded—only to open more doors in the service sector. The trend toward using more health services accelerated. Needs for educational services also increased, as the fast pace of technology mandated retraining of the labor force. The role of financial services grew, and the growing need for banking, pension planning, brokerage, and insurance created new employment opportunities. The process fed on itself. As more people found jobs and their earned income increased, the demand for a whole new variety of services also increased.

At the corporate end, the office of the future justified the use of computers, software, accounting, legal, and consulting services. The information revolution that accompanied the early phase of this transition concentrated on hardware design. As the process of change continued, so did the need for hardware production, software interfacing, and services. Retraining of the labor force through seminars and targeted

Figure 7–1. Employment in the Postindustrial Society

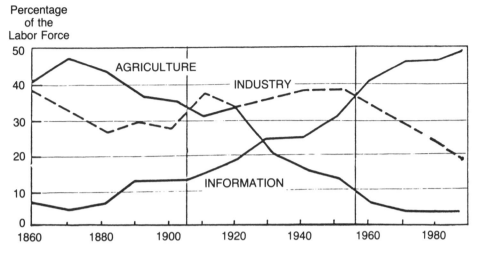

Source: The Commerce Department.

courses became an integral part of the proliferation of technological innovation in the workplace.

There are several key differences between the manufacturing and service sectors. In manufacturing, labor unions were able to mandate their demands on management, but they may have more difficulty doing so in a service environment. Their action is partially paralyzed by the service sector's fragmentation and lack of uniform job specifications. Furthermore, deregulation and intense price competition make it difficult for militant unions to emerge in the service sector.

While manufacturing cannot escape its destiny of automation, the service sector will benefit from technology by improving productivity without limiting available job opportunities. The service industry should continue to evolve into more efficient applications—but only if manufacturing and technological innovation provide it with the means to progress in that direction.

For example, point-of-sale terminals in supermarkets and electronic funds transfer in banking illustrate the point. In both cases, the efficiency derived from organizing the service process depended on technology. In the case of the supermarket, the one-on-one relationship that once prevailed in the local grocery store was lost. The introduction of efficient technological cashier techniques has added further to that efficiency. In the case of fast-food restaurants, technology used in the kitchen during order preparation has allowed the prompt delivery of products. In the case of automated banking, human interface has almost been eliminated, except for errors in accounts. All problems have been pooled in a central location, where they are resolved. Other examples in the service sector where technological innovation has mushroomed include credit card applications, car washes, coin-operated machines, and all sorts of computer-based point-of-sale and inventory control methods.

In most service industries, startup costs are large, and competition is fierce. Unlike manufacturing, services are not protected by patents or other technological innovations. Instead—due to their lower profit margins and the importance of strategic location—they could become the privilege of large operators. Large startup costs prohibit new entrants from competing effectively.

The service sector should continue to expand in the future and discover more efficient methods of mass-marketing services in a dynamic society. However, it should also continue to be dependent on manufacturing and technological applications. The main drawback of the service sector is that it is plagued by low productivity unless it relies on machines and minimizes human involvement with the services rendered. In that case, we should not expect it to grow as quickly as it has in the past, absorbing new entrants into the job market. Moreover, the service sector will maintain an inferior income level compared with manufacturing, as long as the duties performed do not require a high level of skill.

In sum, the service sector will always continue to exist, although we doubt that it can stand alone as a sole provider of economic growth. If war erupts, the service sector cannot defend the civilization that we hope to build around it. This leads us to conclude that we have to revitalize our manufacturing base, invest in R&D, and continue to pursue our drive for more advanced technologies. Manufacturing is here to stay, no matter what form it may take. Service, all by itself, is unable to create new sources of wealth. History tells us that only manufacturing and technology could bring to mankind in one century what the service sector failed to deliver since the beginning of time.

THE GREAT EXODUS: "MADE BY AMERICA ... IN MEXICO"

Offshore manufacturing, or global sourcing, defined as a more efficient use of worldwide resources of labor, materials, and capital, dates back to over a century ago. As early as 1867, Singer Corporation established a manufacturing facility in Glasgow to produce sewing machines. With the fast economic growth after World War II, multinational corporations emerged as a major force in the global economy. At the beginning, the success of manufacturing abroad was based on cheaper labor costs and an abundance of natural resources that entered into the final product.

During the 1960s, multinationals were able to integrate their global production capacity such that each performed only those aspects of the manufacturing process in which it had a superior advantage. Managerial and technological decisions were organized by the parent company to link the subsidiaries into a unified production process.

In the seventies, mounting pressure for short-term performance, intense competition from the rising Far East, ambitious demands of militant unions, the oil shocks, inflation, the humble job experience and education of the baby boomers, and the overall slowdown of global economic growth compelled U.S. companies to restructure and to seek cheaper sources of manufacturing.

Now over 45 percent of our imports are products manufactured for U.S. corporations overseas. In pursuit of lowering their production costs, companies have transferred their manufacturing base abroad. Final goods are now produced in Mexico, Brazil, South Korea, and Singapore. They are then imported to the domestic economy for consumption.

In sum, offshore manufacturing has grown to alarming extremes that threaten our future as an industrial country and as a leader of the free world. The voices of those who advocate trends in social development welcomed this shift as a promising advance toward the service society of tomorrow. The idea seemed attractive for a while, but the realities of the outcome made us wonder about its strategic viability and its impact on our future control of our own destiny. Offshore manufacturing led to the hollowing of corporate America, the transfer of jobs to foreign countries, the export of our technological know-how to other nations, the loss of control over our industrial resources, and the decline of our future manufacturing capability. The long-term implications of this massive exodus of U.S. corporations to offshore manufacturing facilities could have a devastating effect on our standard of living. It is writing off our chances to revitalize our industrial base and to regain our competitive superiority.

On one hand, U.S. employment in manufacturing has plummeted over the past two decades. In 1987, less than 18 percent of total jobs in the domestic economy were provided by the manufacturing sector, declining from 34 percent in the late sixties. The service sector absorbed not only those displaced from manufacturing, but also all the new entrants into the job market. This was at the expense of lower income per employee. After adjusting for the roaring inflation of the seventies, real income and purchasing power suffered, and the standard of living declined substantially. While that lower standard of living has been partly compensated for by the two-paycheck society, its net impact on overall economic growth would be felt during periods of recession, when unemployment rises.

Moreover, with offshore manufacturing, we are cheaply giving away the results of our discoveries and our technological know-how to foreign entities. It takes us several years and millions of dollars to develop an idea from the R&D laboratories into a commercially viable product. Then, we help foreign manufacturers to develop the local expertise of their engineering base, only to find out later that they produce our products cheaper, claim their superiority in quality, and flood our markets. Our experience with the Japanese and the newly industrializing countries (NICs) has proven to be just this.

One case in point is the consumer electronics market. After our decisive superiority during the 1950s in this market, we gave it away to the Japanese in the sixties and seventies. U.S. television and audio manufacturers have surrendered totally to the Japanese invader. Similarly, we developed the video recorder business, yet we lacked the infrastructure to produce it when mass marketing became feasible. Instead, we relied on the industrial samurai to fill our needs in that lucrative and growing market.

So, while we are complaining about our lack of productivity, we are not giving the skill of our labor force a chance to develop. We are denying ourselves the chance to develop our domestic technical base of expertise and skilled labor. In time, we will be left unable to compete because we will lack the necessary industrial infrastructure.

There is no doubt that manufacturing in other parts of the world allows us to benefit from the cost structure and cheap labor in those economies. We can also cite the benefits of international cooperation toward achieving our political and social goals; global manufacturing allows the LDCs to boost their national income and to pay their debts. But when we face a mass exodus of our industrial might to other parts of the world, we can expect offshore manufacturing to work against our long-term interests.

We cannot yield to dreams of a promising service society. We should not aspire to make more hamburgers, drive more trucks, and operate more cash machines. This is not a viable solution to maintaining our standard of living and our leadership in the world. Our comeback to prosperity and growth must be based on maintaining our industrial base at home. We should strive to reindustrialize our domestic economy if we are to regain control over our national wealth.

A COMPANY AND ITS BELIEFS—THE LEGEND OF IBM

What do you do if you are in your mid-fifties and about to enter the turbulent 1930s? That was the challenge that Thomas J. Watson undertook. Indeed, he built IBM, the bluest of blue chips ever established. To the free enterpriser, it represents entrepreneurship at its best. To investors, IBM is the soul of the stock market. Thomas Watson was able to turn an unknown industrial scales and clocks company into the largest computer company in the world. How did he do it?

During the early years of the depression, IBM landed a large contract from the Census Bureau. In the wake of the passage of the Social Security Act in the mid-1930s, IBM was granted a large government contract to supply the accounting equipment needed. The technology of the day was mainly sorters and punch-card machines. Bulky electromechanical relays and counting wheels processed census data and payrolls.

While other companies were laying off people, IBM was expanding. IBM had a phenomenal growth rate of 22 percent during 1945–1955 and 16 percent during 1955–1970. The company has been able to operate at a very high profit margin during its entire history. IBM's Far East subsidiary maintains almost 30 percent of the mainframe computer business in Japan. IBM has proven time and again that it is able to protect its own domestic market and to compete on a global scale.

Thomas Watson was a sales genius, an administrator par excellence, and an innovator in the then-new science of management. He retired at the age of 82, leaving behind a giant company in an infant industry. His son, Thomas Watson, Jr., headed IBM from 1955 to 1971 and further contributed to the work of marvel that his father started. The company then evolved from a centralized management under his father to the modern decentralized business it is today.

IBM's success was based on three basic tenets of its corporate culture. First, successful marketing of both the product and follow-up service played a key role in the phenomenal growth of the company. At IBM, the customer comes first. Since its inception, the company has adopted a policy of responding to clients' needs with the utmost of professionalism. However, customer satisfaction has long been a tradition in America. It is the backbone of our excellence. It creates the image, trust, and continuity of the mission of any enterprise. It brings referrals and carries brand names to the highest pedestals of esteem. It enhances the name of a corporation far beyond where advertising dollars could reach. It delivers a message to the rest of society: *We care.* That was the secret of success that Thomas J. Watson diligently abided by, and it worked.

IBM's success was also based on its respect for the individual. Employees at IBM are allowed to exercise their entrepreneurship and enterprising potential during their lifetime careers. The company has managed to grow from within and promote from within since its early days. It proved to the world that paternalistic companies that weather bad times with minimal layoffs could grow and prosper. The older generation of IBMers set the example of professionalism; in those days, wearing white shirts was mandatory. And work days began with company songs.

The third core belief at IBM is the pursuit of excellence. Today, quality and competitiveness are cited as the main reason behind the legendary success of Japan. At IBM, that has been the way to go about business from the start. It is clear that consistency of a bone-deep belief in excellence yields fruitful results.

Today, IBM is very different from what it used to be; managing growth has shaped the company's method of operation. Yet its culture is the same and continues to be the reason for its success. IBM contributed to university research, built schools, and offered the world the talents of great entrepreneurs that came from its rank. Gene Amdahl, the founder of Amdahl Corporation; Jesse Awaida, one of the founders of Storage Technology; and others came from IBM. This company is a pioneer in robotics and the largest manufacturer and user of semiconductors in the world.

It may be that the Japanese corporate culture, with which we are fascinated today, finds its origin at IBM. Diligent, hard-working, and talented individuals promote the business of the paternal organization, which affords them a secure living. It may also be just a coincidence; indeed, the generation of entrepreneurs that built IBM were from depression working-class families similar in mentality to the defeated post-World War II Japanese who helped their country to achieve its legendary success.

While we are faced with the dilemma of declining competitiveness and a questionable industrial outlook, we should refer to the story of IBM as an example of what depression-born entrepreneurs have done. Napoleon Bonaparte refused to acknowledge the word "impossible." Although this may have brought about his defeat in the war with Russia, it serves today to show us the value of perseverance, which has been behind every great deed in the history of mankind.

SUPPORT YOUR LOCAL ROBOT

They never complain about working conditions. They are always ready to work extra hours without asking for overtime. They never ask for a raise or a bonus. They do not occupy big offices with expensive furniture. They never argue or claim seniority on the job. They do not have to be motivated. They are never absent and can function perfectly without breaks or vacations. They work under severe environmental conditions. They never threaten to go on strike. They seldom make mistakes and, most important, they hold the answer to the declining productivity of the West. Robots are replacing human labor in manufacturing at an ever-increasing pace.

The economic benefit of using automation in manufacturing is apparent. Consistent production, shift after shift, and quality that is hard to compete with are strong advantages of using robots. Robots come in different sizes and capabilities and can be programmed to perform a variety of tasks. They also communicate easily with other equipment; they can be connected to a personal computer and perform wonders. They can be used beneficially in medicine, mining, chemistry, and deep-ocean research, besides performing tedious, repetitive manufacturing jobs. They also perform well under stressful environmental conditions.

Day after day, the trend is shifting toward vertical integration of manufacturing methods. Nothing is new under the sun; how we dealt with the agricultural industry at the turn of the century is now how manufacturing is going. Employment in the agricultural sector kept sliding after the turn of the century, and its decline accelerated at the onset of the depression.

Today, with competitive pressure for cheaper final goods and products mounting from the Japanese, the Taiwanese, and the Koreans, it seems that automation is one of few options left to the Western nations to help us compete. Relying on other nations to supply us with manufactured goods is not strategically feasible. The way out for industrialized nations is to gradually replace their manufacturing labor force with robotics, even though the process is painful to many. The service sector should absorb those displaced during the process.

Robotics is not a new word. It is derived from the Czech word *robota*—servitude. The early stages of development date back to the 1950s, when Joe Engelberger and George Devol pioneered research in that field. At the helm of Unimation Corporation, after spinning off of Consolidated Diesel Electric, they wrote history as they perfected their machines and innovated ways of using them in manufacturing. They tried to sell their dreams but were met with skepticism.

So they took their ideas to a new nation barely making its presence felt in the international arena; Japan was the first country to believe in the future of robots and to invest heavily in them. The stronger the Japanese economy grew, the more interested corporate America became in Japan's management style. Then, robots were seriously considered as an important option offering effective global competition.

On the verge of serious dislocation in their markets, the automakers, the machine tool manufacturers, high tech companies, and many other industries embarked on a slow process of hiring robots in masses. Initially, this shift was met with resistance from labor unions and the government, as the shadow of high unemployment, which kept rising in the 1970s, haunted them.

However, automation gained management support and became the focus of manufacturing strategies. We had to automate if we were to stand a chance in the competitive manufacturing arena. This transformation is still in progress and should expand until we close the twentieth century. In the future, manufacturers may not have to lay off a large number of workers when inventories of goods exceed demand. In fact, the introduction of robots to the labor force may positively affect the traditional business cycle and the unemployment rate.

Today, Japan is still by far the largest employer of robotics in manufacturing, with a market share exceeding 60 percent of the total robots used around the world. Japanese workers have accepted the automation process more readily than their fellow Americans. They do not object to dusting the robots standing next to them on the production line. Workers' responsibility was extended to take care of the robots and to fix them when they stopped functioning. A Japanese official, asked about the intense competition that Japan is facing from Korea and Taiwan, was quick to answer that the competition will be between Japan's robots and the still-cheap labor in those countries.

IBM is already using advanced automation in its manufacturing plants. Since IBM has no unions, it had no problem in choosing the most appropriate and cost-effective manufacturing methods—without having to worry about collective bargaining. IBM also produces robots that vary in level of sophistication. IBM entered the robotics market in 1982, with a low-cost model manufactured in collaboration with Sankyo Seiki, Ltd., of Tokyo. General Electric is also a serious contender in the robotics field. Westinghouse, which acquired Unimation in 1983, is closely following the top two in the race. Another pioneer in the field is Cincinnati Milacron in

Ohio, which started almost at the same time as Unimation and has not stopped since.

Corporate America's acceptance of and commitment to robotics have been accelerating in the 1980s. The trend should pick up more steam as we enter the 1990s. The advantage that Japan gained by leading in automation is at the heart of the different managerial style that Japanese executives have been using for the past three decades and is the single most important factor contributing to their legendary success. Japanese management is oriented toward long-term growth and has leaned heavily on technology to support its expanding markets. American executives, on the other hand, are oriented toward short-term results and are more inclined to be financially driven. Whereas Japanese workers have accepted automation as a *fait accompli* in the curve of human advancement, we have only recently realized that unless we stay in the race we may risk the total demise of our manufacturing competitiveness.

PREORDAINED PAIN—THE SOCIAL COST OF AUTOMATION

Technology has been the most powerful factor behind our big economic advance since the Great Depression. Mankind has progressed throughout history at a slow pace. However, with the advent of technology, the standard of living grew logarithmically. Technology has added to the quality of life and has afforded us new means and ways to expand our horizon. But there is no free lunch anywhere, and technology is no exception. Society does eventually pay a price.

The rate at which technology creates jobs in the economy is much less than the rate at which it eliminates them. Automation at this stage of our industrial evolution holds the dream of the world of abundance of tomorrow, but at the same time it has been replacing factory workers at a faster pace than society could accommodate. The service sector was able to absorb gradually the displaced and new entrants, but only at lower income levels. Thus, the standard of living and personal income per household declined.

Technology has a deflationary effect on the economy and leads to lower prices. This could partly counterbalance declines in purchasing power, since fewer dollars earned will still be able to buy cheaper products that automation and technology afford us.

To overcome the problem of displaced workers, we have to retrain them to perform other functions in the economy and to assume different responsibilities. For example, the switch from manual to electromechanical telephone exchanges has substantially reduced the number of telephone operators who establish the connection via cords. However, it created new jobs in manufacturing, where those automatic switches are produced. The introduction of computerized switching equipment, which later replaced the electromechanical ones, has further eliminated many jobs but has created new ones that require a higher level of skill.

Not only should the displaced be retrained, but also new entrants into the job market must be trained. Those who will be programming, maintaining, and directing the factory of the future have to command a high level of technical expertise. Managers of the future have to be technologically literate to implement effective strategies. Our educational institutions should accommodate these fast technological changes. Science, mathematics, and engineering literacy will be needed in the future more than ever before if we are to adjust to this new technology. Continuous updating of skills and knowledge will be required. Seminars and continuing education courses will become a necessity, enabling employees to cope with these fast technological changes.

The marriage of telecommunications and computers has revolutionized all aspects of our life, both at home and in the office. The future application of microelectronics, fiber optics, artificial intelligence, and superconductivity will boost manufacturing efficiency and require highly talented employees to operate them. Automation will go far beyond the basic functions of assembly, painting, inspecting, packaging, and warehousing. Flexible manufacturing will even allow a computer operator to use different software programs to produce different products using the same machine.

The mushrooming of technology will most likely also allow more people to perform their work from home. A network of computer terminals would allow employees to hold conferences and to exchange information. Decentralization of work will be the new way of life. Manufacturing will take place around the clock, and finished goods will be affordable and in abundance.

Banking, insurance, retailing, and transportation will also benefit from technology. Faster automatic trains and subways will cut commuting time. Even mail systems will have to evolve to fully automated processes. As a matter of fact, with today's technology, people could have a fully integrated machine that uses telephone lines to exchange messages. The need for hand delivery of mail is more political than technically feasible. The only problem is that this could displace a large percentage of workers in the post office. It would be necessary to retrain those masses to perform other functions, which is not easy to do without unemployment soaring briefly. Progress in machine voice recognition will make this process simpler and faster.

In sum, we face a series of hard decisions in the years ahead. To automate or not to automate? In the early 1970s, we wanted to slow down the pace of our progress and pay more attention to a healthier environment. Then came Japan Inc., which drove the whole world to the wall. For Western economies to recapture their lost market share, we have to devise ways to produce products more efficiently and at lower prices.

We thought about manufacturing in other countries, where the cost of labor is lower. Then we realized that we were transferring control over our valuable R&D and technological resources to foreign nations. We found out that once they develop their knowledge base and their industrial infrastructure, they invade our markets but close theirs to our products.

We finally realized that reindustrialization is our answer for a strong America. We also accepted that manufacturing has to survive in parallel with the service sector. The factory of the future is in the process of evolving gradually.

Once automation is in full swing, we will be faced with a different issue. In the past, we were concerned with the creation of wealth and production. In the world ahead of us, the challenge will be how to distribute that wealth, given the number of people who will be displaced from their jobs and who will not be able to adapt to retraining for more sophisticated tasks. The distribution of the pie of abundant manufactured goods produced by automation becomes the challenge that we will take in the 1990s and beyond. Who determines who gets what? Is it going to be a world of programmers and engineers? What will happen to those who cannot be trained to perform functions that go beyond simple assembly? No one has the answer, but it is important to recognize the existence of that challenge over the next few years. Creating jobs to employ those displaced by a fully automated manufacturing system is a challenge that both the administrators and business have to face.

WHAT DOES AMERICA NEED TO COMPETE?

The question has been asked time and again: Can America compete? The decline in our manufacturing effectiveness has led some observers to doubt our ability to come back. They claim that the United States is closely following the trail that led to the decline of Great Britain earlier this century. But America *can* get back on track toward efficiency and can compete. The road to safe shores simply requires awareness of the origin of our problems and the winning spirit to tackle them.

We have to devise our corporate strategies with our eyes set beyond short-term considerations. We have to stop managing with a trader's mentality and opt to be long-term investors in value. We have to position ourselves for future appreciation, rather than speculate on immediate results. We have to manage as if tomorrow matters and stop blaming the world for unfair practices. We have to take analysts' quarterly reports as a grain of salt and focus our efforts on growth potential. We have to invest in R&D. We also have to upgrade the skills of our labor force so that they can cope with the fast changes of technology. Learning is a lifelong trip that never ends if we are to continue to progress.

We have to earn our standard of living and stop borrowing from abroad. A more promising future is attainable by increasing our productivity. We have to be proud of our work and our products. We are still the envy of the whole world and an example of excellence. What we have suffered from over the past few years is complacency, which has caused some economic hardships and gotten us to spend more than what we earn. We have to rethink our buy-now-and-pay-later mentality. We have to save more and invest more.

We cannot rely on the service sector alone to achieve all those objectives. It is much more difficult to create wealth without manufacturing. It is even more difficult to export our services. The industrial renaissance of the next century will be based on fully automated techniques. It will bring our world closer to the new frontiers of unlimited abundance. But we have to prepare ourselves for new challenges, as the factory of the future requires highly skilled employees. Instead of shying away from competing with the industrial samurai, we have to persist and compete. We have to stop shifting our industrial base to far-off lands and relocating our technology abroad. America's return should be made a national goal. Our people should be made aware of our goals to recapture our economic superiority.

Free trade should be an objective to strive for rather than a prescribed course of action. Foreign competitors have a natural advantage of cheap labor which would cost us our standard of living if we were to match it. Dumping by foreign exporters should be stopped, and unfair trading should be opposed. We should revise our antiquated trade practices and replace them with bilateral negotiations to reach equitable terms.

Excellence in manufacturing depends on three factors: price, quality, and service. We can compete in price, and we have the foundation to produce the best quality in the world. Our tradition of excellent services has never changed in face of the challenges of the recent past. But we have to go back to basics and provide customers with that little extra that makes the difference. Efficiency never left America. It was just dormant, and the crash of 1987 awoke it violently.

□ 8

The Frontiers of Supertechnology

Toward a World of Abundance

"We have to resist the siren's song of the economists. They do steady-state economics and want everyone to behave as a reasonable economic person. But the world is not made that way. There are economic fluctuations as well as social and political changes that the sweet dreams of the economists cannot encompass. We must expect change, and prepare for change with resilient technologies. Technology is not a separate phenomenon; it is a product of life. We need it to survive and to prosper."

Dr. Lewis M. Branscomb
Vice President and Chief Scientist
IBM Corporation

In less than a hundred years, the industrial revolution has taken mankind to the Space Age. This explosion in technological discoveries is reshaping our life on this planet. It carries the hope of the world of abundance of tomorrow. Our concern about the stock market crash totally ignores the wonder that technological breakthroughs could bring to our future. Our battles with declining productivity could be won if we use technology to boost our efficiency. We should look beyond the horizons if we are to score the ultimate triumph.

Since 1945, this explosion of knowledge, which was partly stimulated by World War II, has taken us to boundless limits. It has accelerated the perfection of manufacturing methods and the industrialization of agriculture. Our productive capacity doubled, our standard of living rose, and our economy grew. The speed of scientific discoveries led to sharp acceleration in the rate of technological obsolescence. In the fifties, we hardly knew the transistor. Yet before we realized its potential, large-scale integration of superpowerful chips became a reality.

The curiosity of the scientist, the ingenuity of the inventor, and the quest of the entrepreneur for profits have brought about a leap in our standard of living at home and abroad. Technology can compensate for lack of natural resources. It also allows mankind to conquer time. From commuting on foot to horseback riding, the automobile, and the airplane, technology now holds the promise of organized space-shuttle trips to other planets. Here in the United States, we feel it, we live it, we cherish it, and we have great expectations for its future. Technology is taking us to frontiers we never believed existed.

From time to time, we encountered the ugly side of technological disasters, which slowed us down from pursuing progress. The Three Mile Island incident in 1979 and the Challenger's loss in 1986 are examples of such crises. The first atomic explosion brought World War II to an end and slowed down our research in nuclear energy. Similarly, nuclear power plant disasters prevented us from searching for alternative sources of energy to end our dependence on OPEC. Scientific accidents at these early stages were discouraging. But the world pressed on. We were always able to overcome our doubts and tame the unknown.

Despite these setbacks, the revolution is still alive, and we have no choice but to exercise our options to their limits. The rise of other countries around the world as mighty contenders to our economic superiority is forcing us to accelerate our quest for new sources of growth. In the late sixties and the early seventies, we wanted to slow down the pace of our life. Back then, we were in a race with ourselves in a world that was trying to rebuild and catch up with civilization.

We replaced our enthusiasm and drive for a higher standard of living with a greater focus on solving the threat of environmental pollution. We neglected research and development (R&D) and became happy with our achievements. We rested on our laurels and thought we could maintain our pace. But the industrialization of other nations around the world challenged our leadership. They shared in our economic wealth. In the eighties, we suddenly realized that we were a debtor nation for the first time since World War II.

Today, our world is on the verge of another great technological revolution that will afford mankind the realization of its sweet dreams. It should help us to recapture our past achievements and to regain our industrial might. Our economic discomforts in the eighties should stimulate our drive to lead the human race into the century to come.

THE FOUNTAINHEAD OF PROGRESS

Since World War I, R&D has been the backbone of industrial and economic prosperity in the United States. It has propelled us to the forefront of world leadership. It has been and will continue to be the source of rejuvenation of our technological and social progress. It has allowed us to harness science and to use it to boost our standard of living. Faced with all the challenges ahead, we have to make a positive commitment to revitalizing our R&D base and to unleashing its power to bring us out of our economic malaise.

In its early days, corporate R&D was concerned with commercial applications. Scientific and exploratory research was left to government and university laboratories. As the domestic U.S. market expanded and corporations grew in size, R&D assumed additional functions. R&D departments gathered information, devised ways to improve current business, and served as educators to the rest of the firm. The government made available existing patents and granted research funds to a large number of companies.

The two decades that followed World War II witnessed an era of significant innovations. Technological discoveries accounted for some 40 percent of the growth in our Gross National Product (GNP). Thanks to the large R&D investment we made, we brought numerous applications to the marketplace. Pharmaceutical research dramatically improved the general health and quality of life of the population. Study of the structure of the atom unveiled the power of nuclear reactions. Discovery of the transistor opened the door to a multitude of applications in telecommunications, data processing, and computer technology.

Corporate management is a continuous process of dealing with risk and future uncertainties. R&D ranks high on that score. A discovery may be technically sound but commercially unprofitable. The payoff is long term by nature, and assessment of success becomes complicated in a fast-changing environment. In the late sixties and during the seventies, capital allocated by manufacturing companies to R&D suffered a serious drop. Inflated expectations led to disappointment, and management grew more frustrated with the lack of results. They felt that R&D had to yield profits immediately. When it failed to do that in the short term, management curtailed its expenditures on research.

Furthermore, in the seventies, government regulations added to the potential risk inherent in the R&D process and prevented managers from committing themselves to an uncertain business environment. Roaring inflation further discouraged long-term investments. The baby boomers flooded the market, and consumption of existing products far outpaced supply. The changing taste of consumers made it more difficult to predict future trends. Sagging productivity prompted savings on overhead costs. Rising pollution control expenditures and falling profits left little room for long-term planning. In sum, all these factors deprived U.S. corporations of funds needed to finance R&D; instead, they relied on acquisition and diversification in their growth plans.

With the decline in R&D and the aggressive Japanese penetration of the U.S. market, the stage was set for the pendulum to swing in the other direction. In the early eighties, corporations and management moved to rectify the situation. Cooperative research among companies and between companies and universities began. Allocation of investments to R&D at the national level began to rise again. In 1987, R&D spending totaled about $130 billion. In fact, from 1980 to 1987, federal R&D expenditures almost doubled. While our research budget is larger than that of any other nation in the world, in total spending, as a percentage of GNP, we rank fourth. We have a great deal of catching up to do after years of neglect of our R&D base. During the past 25 years, our allocation to research has been flat, whereas Japan's commitment has doubled and Germany's has tripled.

Today, we are driving toward discovering new materials of superior quality and durability. The world is now moving forward to use superconductors and artificial intelligence to increase productivity. Discoveries in the field of biotechnology are also being used in agriculture and medicine.

Unfortunately, in the seventies, MBA graduates found their way to the corporate suite. Fewer managers boasted of technical know-how. There was a noticeable shift away from science and engineering in our education system. For R&D to yield desired results, we have to improve our technical literacy. Technical literacy should become a management requirement rather than an option. As we enter the age of the fully automated factory, we should rebuild our base of human resources. Well-trained engineers and scientists hold the key to the effective use of technological innovations. Professionals with multidisciplinary experience are needed to act as a liaison between different specializations. The marriage of technology and other sciences in medicine, agriculture, and industry has created a need for a multifaceted white-collar force. At the management level, technical literacy could stimulate corporate innovation and improve productivity. Future management has to reckon with the most efficient ways of using technology and the speed of its obsolescence. Without a base of technical knowledge, efficiency may be more difficult to realize.

In the years ahead, serious and active commitment to R&D should help us to tame the technological revolution and reestablish our industrial competitiveness. We were challenged in the early sixties when the Soviets launched Sputnik. This issue of national pride awoke us from our complacency. Before the world realized it, we had far outpaced the Russians in space technology. Today, the challenge we face is to regain our competitiveness, and R&D is an important ingredient of our comeback plan. For us to meet the challenge of global competition, we have to move fast toward new frontiers of technological applications targeted at increasing our productivity. The automated factory of the future, genetic engineering, artificial intelligence, and a host of scientific breakthroughs need to be directed toward creating new opportunities and preserving the standard of living we earned in the past.

AUTOMATION IN BANKING

As a case in point of how technical literacy at the executive level can do wonders, meet John S. Reed, chief executive and chairman of Citicorp. He graduated with an engineering degree from Massachusetts Institute of Technology and joined Citibank in 1965. After holding several executive positions at both the domestic and international operations levels, he was ready to make one of the most outstanding contributions in the history of the largest bank in the United States.

Founded by a group of New York merchants and politicians, Citibank opened its doors on June 15, 1812, with $800,000 of paid-in capital. The bank continued to grow for the next 100 years to become the largest U.S. bank in 1919, with $1 billion in assets. During World War II, the international bank's operations were dealt a heavy setback, as several branches in Europe were either liquidated or bombed. The bank recovered after the war and, after 1967, reestablished its dominance in international operations. During all those decades, the chief executives that managed the bank's growth had been bankers.

In 1978, Citibank embarked on another avenue of growth. Consumer banking came under focus, and Reed led the way. The bank introduced automated Citicard banking centers. By 1982, the bank had invested some $500 million in advanced banking technology, when it became the "Citi never sleeps" bank of tomorrow. Citicorp led the way to the frontiers of supertechnology in banking. Instantly, the giant bank won a competitive advantage at the consumer's end. This led to greater internal efficiency, higher deposits, lower costs, and higher profits. Citicorp was able to regain its rank as the largest bank in the United States and one of the top banks on the face of the earth.

What can an engineer do in the executive suite of a major bank? That is the question that Reed answered. He had the bank leap forward into the promising technology of tomorrow. The fact that his educational background is multi-faceted helped him and the bank to make that leap into modernization. His action industrialized some of the services that his gigantic financial institution offered.

While his technical background as an engineer helped him to take Citicorp in another direction of growth, he has still exercised his banking knowledge. In 1987, he was credited with another bold decision on looming default of less developed countries (LDCs). Citicorp led other American banks by accounting for $3 billion of reserves against those loans. While the LDC problem has not been resolved, his decision gave bankers around the world other dimensions to consider in settling the crisis.

This is an example of the future trend in management technical literacy. Adam Smith, the grandfather of capitalism, preached the specialization of labor. Today, our institutions have to reshape their models of management to account for the technological changes that are providing us with many alternatives. There are many large corporations in America that could be helped by a John Reed. Corporations cannot ignore the challenge that fast-moving technology is imposing on all levels of management. The factory of the future needs qualified managers who can understand the limitations of science and can capitalize on the opportunities it can yield.

DREAMS OF THE VIKINGS

The Vikings understood the theory behind propelling objects into space. Yet they could not use it, since the infant technology of the time could not develop a superalloy. Since a spaceship is launched into space at high speeds, the friction of its body against the air generates heat that melts the material used. The creation of superalloys with high melting points made it possible for mankind to invade space. The marriage of a multitude of sophisticated technologies contributed to our landing on the moon. Over the years, progress realized through the science of metallurgy made possible the dreams of the Vikings.

The scientific revolution enabled us to change the molecular structure of matter to create a unique set of properties. Stretchable metals, glass that bends without breaking, and plastic tougher than steel are only a few examples of the variety of new materials that science has created. This new science of manipulating the characteristics of matter has promising potential in manufacturing. These revolutionary discoveries will lead to lighter and more energy-efficient products without sacrificing strength and durability. Advanced materials are still in the development stage, but are gradually finding specialized applications. The competitive edge of future industrial developments will depend significantly on the growth of advanced material technologies. The following are some materials that are currently being researched.

Superconductors are materials that do not resist the flow of electricity. Because of this, they do not result in energy loss when used in electronic devices. By eliminating the heat caused by electrical resistance, they conserve energy and do not need ventilation or cooling. They could be used in the design of smaller and faster computers. In addition, superconductors repel magnetic fields. This makes them suitable for levitated trains, magnetic resonance imaging, and magnetic motors. The U.S. government has identified superconductors as an emerging technology that has great future potential.

Technological breakthroughs have also led to an improved class of advanced ceramics. They are used in the electronics, automotive, defense, chemical processing, and environmental industries. Applications include multilayer capacitors, optical wave guides, catalytic converters, waste water treatment, and valves. They are more resistant to stress and less vulnerable to corrosion and can withstand high temperatures. An exciting application of advanced ceramics that is still in its developmental stage is in the automobile industry. Because of their ability to resist heat accumulation, ceramics could result in great savings if used in car engines. On one hand, their use will eliminate the need for a radiator or cooling system in the automobile. This could result in big cost reductions in the car of the future. They will also lead to lighter and more energy-efficient cars.

There are several promising applications for advanced materials. Plastic cans could replace tin cans currently used for beverages. Fiberglass has found a whole series of applications in the telecommunications field. Fiber optics make it possible to transmit voice and data at very high speeds and in much larger quantities than conventional media such as cables and microwaves. The list of potential applications ranges from faster semiconductors to scratchproof eyeglasses. They should lead to a more efficient use of new products that should save the consumer millions of dollars. The quality of life and safety should continue to rise in the years ahead. Progress in materials engineering should help us in our quest for a clean environment.

THE ULTIMATE TRIUMPH OVER FAMINES

How would you like to eat freshly produced and chemical-free vegetables? Welcome to the world of biofarms, which hold the key to man's ultimate triumph over famines and food shortages. The world is experimenting with innovative ways of growing crops outside mother earth. Experiments have been run on growing plants in nutrient solutions instead of in soil. This is called hydroponics. When this process, like all other strides in technology, reaches its full potential, it will allow people to grow plants anywhere they wish. In cities, in the desert, inside or outside their houses, people will be able to grow vegetables and plants without soil. A sponge can be used to support the root, and a sodium light can replace sunlight. Moreover, the growth process can be accelerated.

At its full potential, biofarming could prevent flooding. It could also lead to self-sufficiency for people living far from the outskirts of large cities. For poor countries in Africa with limited arable land, famines could be prevented. In the future, we may be able to grow any vegetable we want all year round.

The process is still in its embryonic stage and is rather expensive. With time and refinement, the price will go down and the process will be simplified. The promise of biofarms is great. They are but one example of how technology allows us to circumvent natural limitations of the environment. They represent a step forward to the future world of plenty.

THE WONDERS OF BIOTECHNOLOGY

Biotechnology has been used for thousands of years in the fermentation of foods and beverages. It is defined as the use of scientifically engineered biological systems to manipulate the molecular structure of organisms to create new products. It is capable of producing large quantities of rare products and improving their quality. A major breakthrough in biotechnology took place during the seventies and early eighties. This, the development of recombinant DNA technology, has opened the door for several commercial applications in agriculture, medicine, pharmaceuticals, chemicals, and food processing.

In agriculture, it is used in improving plant varieties and nutritional quality. Herbicide-resistant corn and wheat are being tested in laboratories. It is also used in animal health care, in the form of vaccines, growth hormones, and twinning. Vaccines are being prepared to protect newborn calves from a fatal disease known as scours. Growth hormones for cows promise a significant increase in milk production. In the food-processing field, they are used to produce vitamins, non-nutritive sweeteners, enzymes, and to detect food contaminants. Moreover, gene splicing is leading to improved nutrient quality in food plants.

In the medical field, the discovery of the structure of DNA is giving hope to finding a cure for cancer, arthritis, heart disease, ulcers, diabetes, and even aging. In addition, biotechnology is used in medical diagnosis.

In pharmaceuticals, biotechnological techniques are used to produce drugs for the treatment of emphysema, anemia, bone fractures, hypertension, and kidney failure. They are also used to produce insulin, vaccines, antibodies, and human growth hormone. Biotechnology's most promising contribution is in the area of health care. It will improve our understanding of the origins and biochemical pathways of several diseases. Progress in biotechnology is good news for the baby boomers, as it will find cures for rare and difficult diseases. The overall state of health should improve. The life span of our generation may very well increase due to future discoveries.

TECHNOLOGY AND FUTURE TRENDS

In the early part of this century, the United States witnessed a transition from an agrarian society to an industrial one. During that time, employment in the agricultural sector continued to decline. Manufacturing afforded us jobs, real growth in productivity, and an overall rise in the standard of living. The expansion of international trade and the globalization of the world economy led to intense price competition, which shifted the industrial structure to countries that had cheaper labor. Because of our belief in free trade, we kept our market open and suffered a setback in manufacturing.

Meanwhile, the discovery of advanced computerized techniques progressed at a fast pace. With the decline in our competitiveness in the global arena, two choices were left. The first was to manufacture overseas where cheap labor could be found. The drawback of this approach was that it took jobs away from the domestic market and allowed our technology to be transferred to other lands. In the long run, this strategy could lead to a loss of control over our manufacturing base and our resources. The other solution was to gear up and compete. One of the important alternatives available to help us regain our manufacturing competitiveness is automation. But every new technological application is at first slow and costly. In the process, we have to consider our social responsibility to provide jobs for our labor force. In the eighties, it was too costly to go full fledged toward the automated factory of the future. Offshore manufacturing was the solution of the eighties.

However, automation could well be the solution of the future. The baby boomers constitute a large percentage of the population. As they reach retirement age, the labor force will shrink in size. The baby boomers' aging will probably be the best opportunity for the factory of the future to be fully implemented. Those who are now expecting a labor shortage at the turn of the next century ignore the capacity of technology to fill the gap left by the baby boomers.

Automation of our manufacturing facilities has already begun in the eighties. In the nineties, the process should proceed at an accelerated pace as we move back toward competitiveness. No matter what the outcome is, the level of skill needed to operate this new world of automation will be upgraded. This, in turn, places additional responsibility on our universities and educational institutions.

Another solution surfaced in the wake of the dollar decline. The fall of the dollar made investment in America appealing to domestic companies as well as to foreign corporations. Several foreign manufacturers have invested in manufacturing plants in the United States. American companies may now find that domestic manufacturing is more cost effective than building overseas facilities, especially in view of their consequent savings in transportation costs.

Similar to what happened in agriculture, employment in manufacturing has been declining. This decline in both sectors does not imply that they are dying industries, but rather represents the vertical integration of their resources. This, in turn, allows the realization of much higher efficiency levels. The service sector will continue to provide the bulk of employment in society. To be more specific, the information society will continue to grow. Technological literacy and expertise are the most important requirements that we have to prepare for. But agriculture and manufacturing will continue to exist in an efficient structure that will provide us with our needs.

MANUFACTURING TO GO

To regain our competitiveness, our companies' only choices are to automate and to make strides toward technological discoveries. U.S. firms have already been investing in flexible manufacturing systems (FMS) and industrial robots to increase productivity, reduce cost, improve quality, enhance profitability, and regain their market share. Automation is not a new concept. The largest robot in the world is the mammoth telecommunications network that ties together the globe. At the beginning, telephone connections were made by operators who had to physically connect the two parties involved. Over time, technology led to the full automation of the telecommunications process.

FMS is the use of controlled industrial robots to manufacture more than one product. By using different software that fits each specific manufacturing process, FMS makes possible the production of different products by the same automatic machine. For a worker to do that, intensive and costly training in different disciplines would be required. The use of FMS helps to reduce inventory, shorten the lead time of production, maximize machine utilization, enhance quality, and ensure management's control of the manufacturing process. FMS is used in the automobile and aerospace industries. It commands a high price and is suitable for large-volume manufacturing with several mixes of parts. FMS also requires extensive facilities preparation and in-house training. Because of its high cost and the required level of skill of operators, it has been growing at a slow pace. However, in the future, FMS will be part of large computer-integrated manufacturing systems.

A cheaper alternative to FMS is industrial robotics. Robotics is a relatively young industry. It has significantly expanded since 1984. Some robotics applications have already helped to boost productivity by 20–30 percent. The use of robots in manufacturing eliminates variations in quality that result from different skill levels of human workers. It also helps to reduce the work-in-process and accumulated inventories. The Japanese have attributed their success in manufacturing to the "just-in-time" production system; with robotics, this system is fully utilized, with the benefit of inventory control.

In the eighties, robots have been used in material handling, machine tool loading and unloading, arc welding, assembly, painting, die casting, inspection, and testing. Robots have also been increasingly used to provide feedback about the environment. This is particularly useful in hazardous locations, such as undersea research and exploration.

The robots of the future will be more powerful, accurate, and speedy. Vision, touch, range, and force sensing will enable robots to make simple decisions. Superconductors and fast computers will help them to handle highly sophisticated operations. Voice recognition and improvement in their communication will further simplify the interaction of operators with them. Eventually, robots will reach a stage at which they will repair and even assemble other robots.

Tomorrow's technology is here today in research laboratories. Technology will continue to fulfill its promise to mankind. It will afford us a continuity of comfort. It carries the hopes of our future generations for a better life and a higher standard of living. It should relieve our worries about needs and chronic shortages. Technology creates new oppor-

tunities and takes away outmoded practices. It opens doors on promises in the future and closes others that yield fewer gains. When tamed and targeted to serve our needs, it has the potential to solve our problems and compensate for our inadequacies. However, we have to invest in technology if we are to reach the frontiers of utopia.

❑ 9

The Road to Globalization

"If two countries which trade together attempted, as far as was physically possible, to produce for themselves what they now import from one another, the labor and capital of the two countries would not be so productive, the two together would not obtain from their industry so great a quantity of commodities, as when each employs itself in producing, both for itself and for the other, the things in which its labor is relatively most efficient. The addition thus made to the produce of the two combined constitutes the advantage of trade."

John Stuart Mill
Principles of Political Economics, 1848

International trade was early favored by David Ricardo, who preached the benefits of free trade. In the middle of the nineteenth century, John Stuart Mill fostered the concepts of his predecessor and cited the efficient allocation of labor and capital that stems from the exchange of goods and products among nations.

However, the Great Depression resulted in a trade war among nations and a collapse in international business activities. The painful consequences of the "beggar thy neighbor" policies of the 1930s necessitated an agreement on the terms of international trade. The Bretton Woods Conference in 1944 established the foundation of today's international economic system. The World Bank was created to provide developing nations with badly needed capital. The International Monetary Fund (IMF) was founded to act as lender of last resort to industrial nations. Those international financial institutions strengthened multilateral cooperation and paved the way for the economic order that governs global trading today. In 1948, the General Agreement on Tariffs and Trade (GATT) was drawn up to ensure that tariff practices were nondiscriminatory and to monitor the compliance of most nations with the rules of free trade.

Since the mid-fifties, the world's economy has been undergoing a transition that has brought nations closer together. The decades that followed World War II witnessed an era of unprecedented expansion in world output and international trade expansion. New technologies fueled an explosion in economic growth. The liberalization of global trading brought about an integration of world economies. The advent of efficient means of transportation and telecommunications quickened the pace of global industrialization. The jet airplane shortened the distance between countries and cut travel time. Expansions in telecommunications allowed companies to coordinate efficiently their worldwide strategies. Moreover, the explosion in information exchange helped to unify consumers' tastes around the globe. The rise of mammoth multinational corporations further facilitated the flow of technology and manufactured goods among different nations and reinforced international cooperation. In sum, from 1950 to 1985, manufacturing exports worldwide grew over 14-fold.

World trade has contributed to the economic growth and prosperity of both developing and developed nations. Comparative advantage allowed nations to specialize in the production of goods that they could export to the rest of the world at the cheapest prices. The integration of the global economy also focused on improving the welfare of poor nations and facilitating their access to the rich markets of industrialized countries.

The turbulent seventies, however, gave way to serious trade problems. Runaway inflation, skyrocketing interest rates, awesome surpluses accumulated by OPEC, rising structural unemployment in the West, heavy and alarming debts of less developed countries (LDCs), the reign of Japan Inc. over the world markets, and strains of stagnating growth worldwide inflicted serious imbalances in international trade and revived the forces of protectionism. Faced with a shrinking economic pie and a sluggish outlook, countries have imposed barriers on imports. The resurgence of economic nationalism has encouraged policies of nontariff barriers (NTBs). Protectionism is spreading and threatening to interrupt international collaboration.

Because of profound changes in international economics and finance, the world is very different from what it was at the turn of this century. To digest the constraints imposed on our domestic economy, we should stand back and take a broad view of the international landscape. We can no longer hope to resume our growth and resolve our economic difficulties without understanding the exogenous forces currently at work.

The world is evolving, and the United States is at its center. The old view of a world dominated by two superpowers is no longer sufficient to anticipate changes in the economic and social outlook. Over the past few decades, the European Economic Community, Japan, OPEC, and other international organizations have emerged as important contributors to decisions with a direct impact on financial markets. Global interdependence has become a reality, and international economic problems have grown more complex.

FIRST JAPAN ... AND NOW THE NICS

One of the most important developments over the past two decades has been the rise of Japan as a tough competitor in the international trade arena. In a growing economic environment, the pie is large and mild trade imbalances among nations are tolerated. The real problem appears when trade deficits reach unsustainable levels in a stagnant global economy. Japan built its supereconomy by pursuing an aggressive, export-driven economy. We thought that the rise of the yen against the dollar would slow down their aggressive attempts to monopolize the world market. What we have discovered, however, is that we are now possibly facing four *new* Japans.

The world knows them as the newly industrializing countries (NICs). Their surge to prominence as international competitors coincided with the rise of the industrial samurai. South Korea, Taiwan, Singapore, and Hong Kong emerged as the four new shoguns of the global economy. They are the stars of the free enterprise of the progressive Far East. Their economic and political importance is reshaping the balance of power of world trade. They are flooding the market with low-priced products of reasonable quality. In addition, they are amassing a respectable trade surplus. They are presenting Japan with the manufacturing challenge that the West lost. More important, they are following the same strategies that Japan used to gain market share in the United States and around the world.

In the early sixties, manufactured goods represented 15 percent of the total exports of the NICs. In the eighties, these products leaped to over 90 percent of their exports. Over the last 20 years, their machinery exports as a percentage of total exports grew from a scant 5 percent to over 30 percent. Their gross domestic fixed investment has doubled since the early sixties. This phenomenal economic growth has resulted from a healthy increase in both exports and investments.

Their success in the international arena may be due to their openness to Western culture. It may also be due to their governments' intervention policies in the marketplace. But one thing that all observers agree upon is that the price is right. Close government-industry coordination of national economic goals, accompanied by public investments to promote competitiveness in desired sectors, has characterized their establishment of trade superiority. Selective import protection, especially at the early stages of development of the industrial base, was apparent in most cases. Moreover, their governments often played an important role in coordination and acted as information clearinghouses.

Their proximity to fast-growing Japan has given their economies a significant boost upon which they capitalized. The rise of the industrial samurai has had a dual impact on their manufacturing capability: On the one hand, their exports to Japan injected liquidity and allowed them to invest in developing their own internal economies. On the other hand, they imported the advanced Japanese technology and from there developed their own knowledge base.

Access to Western markets—especially the broad U.S. market—has helped those countries to overcome the initial and most critical stage of their industrialization. America has greeted the NICs with admiration for their hard-working and competitive spirit. With a flawless track record as a model of free-enterprise economic development, we even granted them special duty-free privileges. They were included in a program known as the "Generalized System of Preferences" which the United States devised to help developing nations. Under this program, some 140 countries were exempted from about $15 billion of duties in 1987. We stretched a helping hand to unrelenting competitors eager to inflict trade imbalances wherever they went.

In the process of invading the world trade arena, the NICs deprived several LDCs of a fair chance to export and to pay back their debts to American banks. In addition, they closed their markets for so long. Japan itself is using these economies as a base from which to continue its aggressive export strategies. For all we know, Hyundai sounds very similar to Honda. Could it be that Honda has acquired a way to disguise itself and thereby avert trade barriers? Could it be that Hyundai is owned by Honda and that the Japanese are coming through the back door for a change? It is hard for us to verify the answers to those questions, yet they are food for thought.

While Japan is struggling to adjust to the yen shock, the NICs are gaining a leading position on the international trade scene. They are perceived by other economies as providers of cheap products, but they are not yet recognized for superior quality. If the United States does not act now to revitalize its industrial base, they may gain that quality status. Unless sincere efforts are spent to slow down the NICs, the world may wake up one day to find four new, overly successful Japans on its door step.

HANDICAPPED BY THEIR OWN CHOICE

At the opposite extreme from the NICs are the LDCs. Their economies are driven by exports of raw materials and natural resources. The majority of them suffer from fast growth in their populations. Free enterprise is preached, but seldom followed. They suffer from low productivity, modest skill of their labor force, and a great deal of undefined political ideology. Politics overrules economic considerations. Their people are stricken by poverty and are deprived of their born right to choose freely their destiny. Dictatorship is followed by dictatorship. Freedom of the press, in some instances, goes as far as publishing only what the governing body wants to relay to their people. The LDCs are constantly asking for aid from the rich Western nations, and whenever they are denied it they talk about communism.

Resistance to change is blamed for the way they perceive the globalization process and the role that their countries could play in it. They hesitantly accept cooperation with multinationals. They believe that foreign-owned enterprises do not have any allegiance to LDC economies and that they are solely pursuing profits from their global production and sales.

They ignore the fact that these large enterprises command huge resources and can take risks that their domestic companies cannot afford to take. Eventually, these resources flow back into their own economies in the form of broad-based improvements in the skill level of their own people. They also forget that the manufacturing and sales processes inevitably lead to the development of new products and services that their economies need. Moreover, techniques used to manage those enterprises lead to a sophisticated and modern institution, which will also eventually benefit their development.

LDCs also accuse multinationals of monopolistic tactics that prohibit local enterprises from growing. They forget, however, that their governments could initiate legislation to protect local industries. That legislation, however, should not impede foreign enterprises from executing their production and financial goals. They should also remember that each government intervention increases the costs, complexity, and risks assumed by foreign enterprises. This could eventually lead to reassessment of the viability of investing in such a country, which holds the risk of total withdrawal of foreign investors.

THE IMPEDIMENT TO PROGRESS— INTERNATIONAL DEFAULT

One of the most disruptive developments challenging the progress of the world economy is the inability or unwillingness of LDCs to pay back their loans. Third World countries have been living on borrowed time. The industrialized nations believe that prudent economic management by the LDCs could bring the world closer to cooperative exchange. Yet every time we hear about a revolution in the Third World, we hope for a positive change that does not materialize. Experience has shown that prospects do not improve, and often enough they regress.

The looming international default on LDC loans is a case in point. During the heydays of the 1970s, it was believed that sovereign nations could not go bankrupt. It was thought that their rich commodity resources and improved balances of payments would bail them out and allow international lenders to recoup their funds. But inflation subsided and economic growth slowed worldwide. Yet LDCs either stopped servicing their debts or limited their payments to a low percentage of their export revenue. Lenders learned that sovereign nations may fail to live up to their obligations. And international banks cannot exercise their claims to assets that are within debtor countries' jurisdiction. Under such circumstances, their only recourse is patience in negotiating those loans for years without end.

When the shadow of default appears, international lending order is reinstated when the IMF requests the defaulting country to balance its trade account. Its currency is devalued, and its productive resources are reoriented toward exports. This, in time, will generate a trade surplus, which will allow the country in question to pay its dues. The process is tedious and long-term. In the interim, the shareholders of the lender bank suffer as write-offs are taken against the loans in question.

The readiness of international banks to extend loans to LDCs is usually based on LDC creditworthiness, regardless of their ability and even willingness to pay at a future date. Debt services are usually paid only if borrowing nations are allowed access to new loans. When access to such loans is threatened, the possibility of total default becomes a reality. Although banks could seize the borrowing country's assets abroad, in real life they never do. Peru defaulted in the 1920s on a $60 million loan, but banks are still lending to that country today. Banks will continue to lend to overseas countries even after they default. Such policies are a vital part of the international political environment.

Our banks will continue to provide loans to the LDCs regardless of the outcome. If we deprive LDCs of a fighting chance, their collapse will have an even more expensive impact on the global economy. As mankind continues on its path toward the future, nations will learn to survive together and respect each others' needs. LDCs are a large market that industrial countries cannot ignore. The recycling of wealth around the globe is an integral part of a world that is still searching for better terms of understanding.

GAMES NATIONS PLAY

The shrinking economic pie in the eighties has forced nations to support import policies and resist each others' exports. With the GATT policing international trade markets, countries have resorted to NTBs or disguised protectionism to protect their own markets and to save jobs for their own people.

Nontariff barriers can take several forms. They can be based on specified quotas of a quantity or type of import. They often take the form of a gentlemen's agreement when presented as voluntary export restraints. Another disguised way of implementing NTBs is through government subsidies of import-competing products and of exporting. They can be effected via export rebates and complex financing privileges extended to exporters. In addition, NTBs can be imposed under the excuse of health, quality, or industrial standards. Finally, they can be imposed via countervailing duties, antidumping rules, prohibitions, embargoes, ownership rules, shipping codes, information controls, currency restrictions, or any combination of the above.

NTBs are very hard to detect, control, and deal with. They are relatively easy to implement and difficult for other countries to prove as violations of free trade agreements. No international regulation has proved effective in dealing with them. They are easily defended as an integral part of national interests, without carrying a convincing argument. Exporters welcome NTBs, which deprive their foreign competitors of access to their domestic market and allow them to dump their products on others.

NTBs have replaced traditional trade barriers and have substantially undermined the free flow of goods and services around the globe. They act as a temporary safeguard to resolve trade imbalances, yet in the interim they inflict great damage to the progress of globalization. In the short term, they provide assurance to people that their government is doing something to stop foreign invaders. However, they grow beyond a country's interests. Every nation is entitled to protect promising industries from well-seasoned multinationals. The problem is when blind and nondiscriminating NTBs are imposed.

Protectionism has important repercussions regardless of the shape or form it takes. It discourages multinationals from dealing with nations that adopt such policies. This step alone deprives those nations of the benefits that cooperative exchange yields—both technologically and economically. Protectionism always results in a loss to the consumer, who has to bear extra costs. Moreover, protectionism restricts the available quality and quantity of goods in the marketplace. It gives a free hand, in most cases to local producers, regardless of their efficiency or quality. At times, it leads to shortages and regression in the upgrading of products. In addition, it encourages complacency of the protected labor force and prevents it from acquiring the skills needed to compete. All said, protectionism is an impediment to the free exchange of knowledge and information among countries around the globe, without necessarily bringing home the benefits it is intended to.

The emergence of NTBs in the eighties has expanded due partially to the aggressive trade strategies that Japan and the NICs have pursued. In a shrinking world economy, countries had little choice but to stop the bloodbath that the Japanese market share inflicted on domestic producers. The problem that resulted from such developments is that NTBs were applied indiscriminately and carried to extremes. Such barriers have ultimately caused world output to decline and carry the threat of trade wars and open retaliation.

REACHING FOR A GLOBAL UNDERSTANDING

The trade deficit has cost our nation a great many jobs, which migrated to foreign countries. We were the leading signers of the GATT, and we stood up to that responsibility. We abided by our beliefs in a world that selfishly pursued its own goals. We sacrificed our markets on the altar of free trade and denied our companies a fair chance to compete. Our policies supported the foreign invasion of our markets, and we bore the brunt of settling for less than first place in the emerging global arena.

We closed our eyes to the Japanese ravaging of our industrial base. Furthermore, with our belief in the spirit of free enterprise, we allowed Japan to exploit our generosity without any reciprocity. We shied away from persevering and competing with the industrial samurai and witnessed the slaughter of other nations in the wide-open and vicious trade arena. Budgets were laden with deficits, and LDCs struggled under the burdens of their debts—unable to meet what they owed our banks. As the LDCs had to defend themselves against the new emerging superpower of Japan, they were prevented from developing their own internal resources.

We cannot blame all on our great multinationals. They were faced with tough choices. They had obligations to their shareholders, which the foreign invaders did not have to meet. They relied on the unlimited resources of entrepreneurial innovation in their organizations to replenish their own market niches. Some could not resist the wave of government-supported and unfair practices that foreign companies adopted. Our multinationals were on their own. Some ended up quitting their traditional markets. Some others decided to compete by relocating jobs, technology, and corporate know-how to far-off lands.

We are not asking for protectionism, and we are true believers in free enterprise. But the time has come to reinstate order in the global market for our own sake as well as for those nations that do not command the power to effect change. We are in favor of fair reciprocity of trade with all nations on the face of this earth. We are the only nation that could take on this challenge. We took this challenge with our neighbors in Canada, and we need to draw up bilateral trade agreements with other Western economies and Japan. They should not get away any longer with their protectionist policies, while they are allowed full access to our markets.

This new global economy could hardly be achieved through a uniform agreement that penalizes those who abide by its principles. It could, however, be achieved via bilateral trade agreements that accept that the responsibility of the Western nations is to continue to encourage the industrialization of LDCs.

While we are pursuing strategies that bring about the free exchange of goods and services, we should make sure that the cumulative inefficiencies that materialized in the past two decades are not repeated. We look forward to a serious and concerted effort from all the nations of the world to cooperate toward reaching that understanding, which should eventually carry a unified people toward the frontiers of greater prosperity.

❏10

The Golden Age of Capitalism

Born in the USA

"You who have been born in America, I wish I could make you understand what it is like not to be an American—not to have been an American all your life—and then suddenly ... to be one, for that moment, and forever after. Think of it. One moment you are a citizen of Armenia, a brave and tiny state out of sight beneath the red tide of Russia. The next, you are an American. One moment, you belong with your fathers to a million dead yesterdays. The next, you belong with America to a million unborn tomorrows."

George Mardikian

The world's economic system was split between capitalism and socialism at the turn of the century. Karl Marx
preached that capitalism was doomed and would ultimately
destroy itself. He thought that the instability of its business
cycle would devastate the greedy world of free enterprise and
that a final crash would leave people disillusioned, providing
a fertile ground for a revolution. He was convinced that
socialism was the only way to reach permanent prosperity.
Well, little did he know!

If not for the free enterprise system, humanity would
have few of the comforts that we take for granted today. Henry
Ford was on time when the United States was about to take a
giant leap from its agrarian past into its industrial future. The
Wright Brothers were bicycle mechanics, yet their spirit of
adventure led to one of the greatest inventions of the century:
airplanes. Graham Bell was an amateur technician. His freedom to experiment allowed the world to communicate thousands of miles apart. Edison invented the electric bulb and

founded General Electric. Thomas Watson built IBM from an unknown scales and clock company in the 1920s into a computer giant. These men and others revolutionized the face of the world.

History tells us that every human disaster left behind great people with great resolve. The miseries of the depression of the 1930s compelled disadvantaged workers to join unions and to support policies that served their interests. Yet despite the suffering and economic devastation of the country, no one favored the formulation of a socialist party. Their capitalistic beliefs eventually were realized as the postdepression era witnessed the age of American greatness.

In the 1980s, Marx's ideology was dealt the worst blow since its inception. Communist country after communist country is now restructuring. They are slowly abandoning the futility of socialism. At the lead are the two superpowers of socialism: Russia and China. Are we witnessing the final triumph of capitalism? What could that mean to the global economy and to our future? Is the world changing around us for good this time? Has the golden age of capitalism finally arrived?

ILLUSIONS OF A COMMUNIST

The communist bloc has practiced command economy since the turn of the century. The government plans and determines for the people what to do, how to do it, when to do it, and where to do it. Total resignation to the state is how they live. People are deprived of their born right to take charge of their destinies. They are denied the chance to profit and to pursue their ambitions. They are modern slaves to government. The lucky ones join the elite governing body; the rest have to struggle accepting the leftovers. They can never hope to build their own enterprises. They cannot voice their resentment because of fear that their neighbors may report them to higher authorities. They live and die without self-actualization. The government allows itself to control their destinies. This is what socialism is all about.

In the Eastern economies, shortages develop frequently. People have to stand in line for a loaf of bread. There are no supermarkets, no Radio Cities, no Broadway shows, no Disneylands, no skyscrapers, and no Wall Streets. The list of "nos" could fill a few volumes. People in such economies are happy just to survive and not be arrested. Creativity is absent.

Everywhere on the face of the earth where freedom was stifled, the economy was chaotic. It is probably true that in socialist countries, unemployment does not exist. However, the standard of living is by far inferior to that of capitalist societies. The levels of satisfaction among people and the quality of life also cannot be compared.

Stalin's brutality made the West abhor and fear the shadow of socialism that dominated the Eastern bloc. In reality, however, Stalin was the proponent of an ill-based economic and social discipline. The experience of socialism in this century revealed the fallacy of the tenet that political democracy could be achieved with a state-controlled economy.

A system that deprives people of their fundamental right to engage in the economic activity of their choice simply could not survive. It could not conceivably establish itself as a way of life without turning into a full-fledged dictatorship. Marx's philosophy could hardly be judged at its inception at the turn of the century. Today, some 70 years later, we can study socialism in experience. Political liberty goes hand in hand with a free economic system, and this is a combination that the world can now verify.

HOW OLD IS CAPITALISM?

Since the beginning of recorded history, man has known only one economic discipline: capitalism. It provided the incentive behind each and every little step of progress that mankind ever achieved. From the discovery of fire to the invention of the automobile, the entrepreneurial spirit was constantly chasing profits. In pursuit of fortunes, individuals' imagination and creativity were set free to perform wonders. There were times when the cost was high. But it was no higher than the cost of wars, famines, and plagues that man endured throughout the evolution of civilization.

Capitalism is based on market supply and demand. You are free to practice business however you like; the market is the final judge. It determines your chances of success or failure. The marketplace balances the excesses without outside intervention. At times, violent cyclical fluctuations in the free enterprise system have led to painful adjustments. When the pendulum swings to one extreme, pain or pleasure is inevitable. And it was through pain that capitalism emerged and prevailed in the twentieth century.

America, the land of freedom, held the banner of capitalism high despite the 1930s. Prior to the sad episode of the 1930s, capitalism was pure. No intervention from any government body took place. The interruption of business activities on the scale of the Great Depression opened the gate for government to play a vital role in business. It introduced many safety nets—balancing mechanisms that reduced the extremity of the business cycle and fostered growth and progress.

Via taxation and even sponsorship at times, the government supported investment in growing sectors that were deemed necessary for the social good. For example, the United States, unlike the rest of the world, has a privately held telecommunications network. While that sensitive business is managed by a privately held enterprise, the service is excellent. Without direct government involvement, our telecommunications industry is run so efficiently that it is the envy of other nations. This is what modern capitalism is all about.

Capitalism goes far beyond the rhetoric of abstract ideologies. The objective record of capitalism in the twentieth century leaves little doubt of its effectiveness as a viable economic system. West Germany is high on the list of such examples. Torn apart after World War II, its economic system, combined with the resolve of a nation to rebuild itself, developed a new industrial might. While East Germany fell behind, struggling with a socialist economy, its other half proved the miracle of free enterprise.

The experience of Taiwan with free enterprise is further proof that oppressive centrally planned economies hinder progress. The People's Republic of China, with ample resources and labor power, fell far behind its neighboring Taiwan. While Taiwan became a model of growing capitalism in the Far East, China suffered years of regression under the false illusion of socialist glory. The result was a swing to the free market system after a perilous experience that lasted over three decades.

In the Western world, the definition of poverty is relative. The working class in capitalist countries enjoys prosperity that is envied by Russia and all the other nations of Eastern Europe. Japan, Taiwan, and South Korea are direct proof of the success of market-driven economies. Russia itself, the leader of all socialist regimes in the world, is highly dependent on the technological progress of the West, which it cannot match.

Capitalism seems to have failed at times, not because of problems inherent in its concept but because of people's ignorance about how it operates. Cycles of pessimism follow periods of optimism. Excesses build through each phase of quantum advance, which lead to prolonged periods of contractions during which capitalism rejuvenates itself. Marx failed to recognize the powerful adaptive capabilities of capitalism. Kondratieff's observations admitted that the free enterprise system endures long-term adjustments rather than a predetermined demise. His admittance of cycles of rejuvenation—rather than doom—sealed his fate in Siberia.

Although capitalism does not guarantee success, it does guarantee the chance and opportunity to succeed. It multiplies the opportunities of financial independence for those who were not born into wealth. It affords all persons in society the freedom to choose the way they want to shape their lives.

In America, many companies, such as Procter & Gamble, Ford, Chrysler, Simon & Schuster, and others are named after their founders. However, under socialism, companies are owned by the government and controlled by government-appointed officials. Great American entrepreneurs who built the largest enterprises in the world would have been prohibited from striving toward their goals if they had been born in a socialist country. They would have been working for a government entity. They would have reported to a government official; in the corporations they founded, they may not have been able to go beyond a supervisory level. The corporations that they built and that employ millions of people would not have stood a chance to exist. Despite all the talk about the decline of the American economy in the 1980s, these companies still rank among the most progressive and sound enterprises—if not the leaders—in the whole world.

As we enter the last decade of this century, the world can better judge the difference between these two economic systems. The resolve of China and Russia to encourage international cooperation is welcome news for global markets. The wave of open door policies should present Western nations with challenges and opportunities to promote further growth. A decline in hostilities between the two superpowers should be celebrated, as it should relieve our economy of the burden of expensive defense expenditures.

SOCIALISM ON THE CHAMPS ELYSÉE

In the wake of the second oil shock in 1979, socialism found its way to the heart of Western Europe and made France a centralized economy. In 1981, President François Mitterand was elected, and the socialists got hold of France. With the help of First Prime Minister Pierre Mauroy, Mitterand embarked on an old-fashioned socialist program that nationalized 28 percent of French industry. He boosted state ownership of business in France to almost 50 percent. This plan imposed heavy taxes on wealth.

At the heart of these socialist reforms was a policy of consumer reinflation to support the initial phase of the transition. The minimum wage was increased by 30 percent, and pensions and social security payments were increased by about 25 percent. In addition, Mitterand and Mauroy succeeded in halting automatic wage indexation. In 1984, for the first time since 1958, hourly wage rates rose more slowly than inflation.

The invisible hand was quick to respond. Inflation doubled during the first year, and unemployment kept rising. France's balance of payments faltered from a surplus of Fr 79 billion to a deficit of Fr 38 billion. In addition, the government deficit ballooned to 3.5 percent of the Gross Domestic Product (GDP). The stock market tumbled. The franc was devalued three times within the European Monetary System. Real GDP remained sluggish, and France missed out on the worldwide economic recovery of the eighties.

Furthermore, the government mishandled several issues, including private schools, the steel industry, and laws on reform of the press. Labor unrest intensified, and demonstrations against the centralized bureaucracy became widespread. Rising taxes and the nationalization of industries and banks led to resentment of the communist left.

The death of excessive government control soon became imminent. In 1981, an alliance of both left- and right-wing parties announced plans to sell government-owned institutions to the public. France finally joined the great movement toward government divestiture of its holdings, which was sweeping the Western world. The British government, under Prime Minister Margaret Thatcher, had already sold the equivalent of $25 billion of its industrial holdings. Similar action was taken in West Germany, Japan, Italy, and even the United States. This came to be known as the greatest deregulation revolution of the century.

The whole great socialist experiment in France was called a big failure as early as March 1983. France, one of the oldest free enterprises of all Western nations, had tasted the sour inefficiencies of a command economy and revolted against them.

Under the direction of Prime Minister Jacques Chirac and Minister of Finance Edouard Balladur, the liberalization movement began. By 1986, the French right was committed more than ever to reversal of the trend toward government involvement in industry and finance. Tax reductions, financial deregulation, and steady reductions of the budget deficit came at the top of the list of reforms. Credit ceilings previously imposed on banks were removed. Over 65 companies were targeted to return to public hands by 1991.

The denationalization of industries in France was here to stay. Even Société Générale, one of the largest banks that was nationalized by President Charles de Gaulle in 1945, did not escape this great reversion to the capitalist movement. Moreover, giant financial institutions, such as Crédit Lyonnais and Banque Nationale de Paris, are also being scheduled for sale.

However, the painful stock market crash of October 1987 halted the process of restructuring in France. The uncertainty of the environment following the crash has seriously challenged this revolution of deregulation. Profits are now expected to slow down, France is not providing banks with fresh capital and those banks have to answer to a large number of small shareholders. The pressing question on the minds of the orchestrators of the privatization program is: Has the deregulation drive lost its momentum? Even more serious is the question of whether banks that are no longer protected by the government are capable of competing in the face of adverse financial conditions.

The future will answer all the questions that the Western world is faced with. We would like to emphasize at this juncture that the trend toward free markets and hands-off laissez-faire capitalism has been gaining strength in the global economy. Despite all its deficiencies, free enterprise has reasserted itself as the most progressive economic system in the world. Freedom to choose cannot be matched by central planning by a few bureaucrats. The pursuit of ambition-driven ends has always built and will continue to build a better world.

AND THE COLOR IS ... RED

Economic and social restructuring has become the dominant characteristic of the 1980s. Major changes in socialist ideology are not only apparent in France, but are reaching deep
into the communist nations as well. These major changes
present the global economy with both a challenge and an
opportunity. The challenge is to ease the pain of the transition
process. The opportunity is to expand cooperation and to
achieve peace and progress. The 1980s are leaving their mark
on the history of mankind.

After seven decades of socialism, the golden age of capitalism is proceeding at its best in this century. Creativity and
entrepreneurship, which were banned and suppressed in the
past, are becoming new slogans. Over with excessive government regulation, over with endless political meetings, over
with ideological futility, over with the drudgery of farmers
team-planting, and over with industrial retardation! That
seems to be the new wave of restructuring that is sweeping
both China and the Soviet Union. This daring and invigorat-
ing spirit is reaching out behind the iron gates of socialism.
The process of crossing the great divide that separates the ideological insularity of the Marxists from the freedom of capitalism is sweeping the globe.

These historic changes promise the world a larger economic pie and expanding opportunities, the likes of which we
may never have seen before. While our world today bears
striking similarities to that of the Great Depression, we should
recognize the boundless global opportunity that could revolutionize our future. A major economic slowdown could
threaten these possibilities for a new world, which holds great
hope for our generation. It could also lead to frustration of
those socialist nations, which are seeking the answers to their
stagnation in capitalism. The world cannot afford to let this
opportunity pass without nurturing its chances to reach its
full potential.

The unrelenting race for armaments may also finally
have come to an end. Hostility between the two superpowers

of the world may have changed into cooperative exchange. The world should celebrate the peace initiatives between the East and the West. Billions of dollars are wasted every year on military procurements.

Peace could help all governments to concentrate their efforts on creating new sources of growth and a better standard of living for their people. Mankind needs to spend more on research to cure AIDS and cancer. We should also strive toward a better environment. We should aim at relieving the agony of hunger that threatens Africa. We should cherish our technological achievements and target them toward creating wealth for future generations.

MASSES ON THE PATH OF REFORM

The People's Republic of China is the third largest country in the world, after the Soviet Union and Canada. Its population is a little in excess of one billion persons, which makes it the most populated country in the world. Its labor force is dominated by the rural sector, 80 percent of which is engaged in agriculture.

In 1949, following the triumph of Mao Tse-tung's People's Liberation Army over Chiang Kai-shek's Nationalists, the People's Republic of China was born. While Mao remained in power until his death in 1976, Chiang was exiled to the small island of Taiwan. And while Taiwan grew prosperous and became a model of emerging Far East manufacturing power, China's economy faltered for decades under socialism.

Thirty-five years later, the leaders as well as the people of China are reaching out to the free enterprise system as a viable economic discipline. In 1977, Deng Xiaoping gained power in the People's Republic of China and embarked on a process of modernization that brought about major economic reforms. The "Open Door Policy" was a new slogan that gradually replaced the socialist "Great Leap Forward." The agricultural sector, which contributes 45 percent of China's national income, was liberalized. Free market policies were allowed in some urban sectors on an experimental basis.

In 1984, the Chinese Communist Party announced liberalized prices, wages, state planning systems, and factory management. Free market forces were allowed to restructure the economy. Growth exploded at 12.5 percent each year, and inflation soared to over 9 percent in 1987. Welcome aboard, China.

In the 1980s, China has been relaxing its working practices, allowing factories to reduce their number of unproductive employees. Also, in 1986, China experimented with new management systems in factories. Reforms stressed financial accountability, enterprise autonomy, superior factory management authority, and less party interference in factory operations. Long-controlled farm prices were removed, and farmers were allowed to sell excess products in the open market. Moreover, a new unemployment insurance system was established.

Substantial monetary expansion in 1979 led to a government deficit. Bond sales and major government expenditure cuts were used to control money growth. By 1985, China was running at a surplus. The highly centralized banking sector was also liberalized, with the state-controlled People's Bank of China acting as the central bank. Foreign banks were allowed to establish offices in Beijing and other major cities and to conduct basic foreign currency and retail banking.

On the import side, Japan was quick to capture the lion's share. In 1986, Japan accounted for 36 percent of China's imports, followed by the United States at 13 percent. One of the major reasons behind this lag in U.S. imports is that China is self-sufficient in agriculture—its demand for our primary commodities is slack. China is more hungry for foreign technology and expertise.

In 1986, China's imports rose only 1.2 percent, while exports grew a brisk 13 percent. Textiles and apparel exports to the United States climbed 63 percent. Export prospects for China to the United States are good as far as computers, telecommunications, energy, electronic instruments, machinery, and packaging equipment.

After years of inefficiency, one should expect change in China to be gradual. Remember that it took Taiwan, only a small island, three decades to spring to the forefront of progress in East Asia. This change in China could even stumble over temporary setbacks. However, the process of change has begun, and there is reason to celebrate one more triumph for free enterprise.

RISING FROM THE ASHES OF OBLIVION

After 35 years of isolation, China removed the straitjackets of socialism and replaced them with modernism. An entire generation grew up deprived of the chance to ride the horseless cart innovation of the twentieth century—the automobile. Bicycles are used in America mainly for exercise; in China, they are used every day to commute to work. A bowl of rice a day and a bicycle ride were the most that Mao's cultural revolution could promise the Chinese people.

The realities of life had to prevail, and the sleeping giant finally said no to the inefficiencies of communism. This century will go down in history as a time when the world experimented with economic ideologies at the expense of forgotten generations in China and other socialist countries around the world. The socialist and communist plague of the century is finally finding a cure, and China is leading the way to it. Indeed, it takes courage from their leaders to introduce such radical changes. China, one of the oldest civilizations on earth, has tasted the disillusion of socialism and has revolted against it.

China has a long way to go. A period of experimentation and development of a new economic system should be expected over the next decade or two. Meanwhile, China has been experimenting with a floating rate currency trading system. The country's operating costs and low productivity are making it uncompetitive for foreign investments. China is in dire need of foreign currencies. Presently, concessions are granted to foreign-owned companies provided that they export to the rest of the world and reinvest their earnings in the domestic market.

China experimented on a limited scale with the idea of establishing a market for stocks and bonds. Even though Shanghai boasted of having the biggest stock market in Asia prior to the 1947 revolution, China's government has been slow to translate its needs to capital markets. Its commitment to transfer state-owned properties into private hands via financial markets has fallen short of expectations.

Also, the Chinese are having trouble in understanding bankruptcy of their enterprises, a result of withdrawn government intervention. They fail to realize that American entrepreneurs often go bankrupt—sometimes more than once—before they hit it big. In China, bankruptcy is dishonorable.

When reforms were first announced, Western entrepreneurs toyed with dreams of quick market penetration. For a while, the rush to China seemed comparable to the gold rush in California. The reality, however, is that the bureaucracy of three decades of isolation has to prevail. Impediments to change are great, despite the sincere willingness of the leaders and the people of China to accept change. Despite its vast potential, the Chinese market is not yet ready for fast growth.

FROM FEUDALISM TO SOCIALISM TO MODERNISM

The transformation process is not easy. Megatrends take time to reach their full potential. At times, fundamental changes lead to instability that could reverse the trends backwards if not tackled delicately. The gratifying rewards of free enterprise can only be realized over the long term. Although China's history has displayed a tendency toward sudden and radical ideological swings, this change promises to be slow.

For one thing, the road back to a free market economy is encountering numerous challenges. Some party leaders across

China are resenting the effect of the reforms on their power over the people. The army fears that change will lead to the loss of its grip over the country. Many old-timers, who had the socialist system working for them, are denouncing the rush of foreigners capitalizing on the vast market potential that China offers.

Undoubtedly, some groups will benefit, while others are expected to be left disillusioned. In 1987, inflation surged to 9 percent; rising prices were attributed by the communists to creeping capitalism. Slashing government subsidies and allowing inefficient enterprises to go under constitute a threat to many of those who are used to the "iron rice bowl," where everybody is guaranteed a job regardless of their contribution. China's resolve will continue for a while to come under internal pressure. Unless economic reforms bring about a definite improvement in the standard of living of the common Chinese, extreme caution could replace their enthusiasm.

China is by no means suddenly the new wonderland. Its standard of living is low. Consumer power is fragile. Red tape and bureaucracy cannot disappear overnight. China's industries are riddled with the inefficiencies of a centrally planned economy. The skill of the labor force is, at best, humble, and illiteracy is widespread. Its market is not developed. Means of communication lag far behind the standards of Western civilization. Cities are congested. The Chinese are ill prepared when confronted with foreign businessmen; their language is difficult to learn, very few professionals in the West have a good command of it, and few Chinese speak foreign languages. In sum, China could take a few decades to reach the sophistication needed to smooth the flow of trade and business.

A whole generation was isolated from the evolution that swept the West after World War II. It is only normal to expect patient strides over a long period of continuous commitment to change. Despite the slowness of change in China, it definitely represents a triumph of free enterprise.

OUT OF HIBERNATION ... CHINA AT THE CROSSROADS

Only the future will tell if China will succeed in its drive toward liberalization of its economy. The uncertainties that surround the conversion process are great, yet we should recognize its potential—a vast market that can open new horizons for world trade.

If China were to surmount the difficulties of shifting its economy toward free enterprise, the global economy would be presented with a new challenge. Japan, Taiwan, South Korea, and other Asian countries proved to be tough competitors in the international arena, and China should be no different. What is happening there is part of a megatrend that will be emerging in our future. The end result could entail expansion in intercontinental trade, which should benefit all countries. Wealth among nations should increase, and the global exchange of goods will add to human prosperity. The triumph of capitalism promises a more peaceful outlook for all countries. It should also pave the way to a healthier exchange of human experience.

THE DAWN OF PEACE ON EARTH

October 1987 is not only the month during which the market crashed, but also the 70th anniversary of the socialist revolution. There are reasons for the world to worry about the meaning of the crash, but also to celebrate the prospect of peace and cooperation with the Eastern communist bloc. The optimist may think that peace on earth is finally within reach and may even hope to witness the ultimate victory of free enterprise. Russia, after decades of military aggression, seems to recognize the virtue of openness and to initiate long-lasting world peace.

On December 8, 1987, President Ronald Reagan and Soviet General Secretary Mikhail Gorbachev signed the first superpower arms reduction agreement in eight years. They gave the world an early Christmas present—hope of a potential reversal in the arms race. Although the agreement covered only minor reductions in medium-range missiles, it should be considered an important step forward in a bigger negotiation process. In fact, these leaders already announced plans for more reductions in nuclear warheads in coming years.

Negotiations between the two superpowers could take a few years. Their goal is a drastic—if not total—reduction of nuclear warheads. Our European allies have reasons to be cautious. They regard the U.S.-Soviet accord and the loss of NATO's medium-range deterrents as threats to West Germany. They are also wary of Russia's superior conventional forces, whose reduction will be hard to negotiate.

The real question comes down to trust and credibility. Should the world have faith in the Soviet initiatives? Or is this a temporary interruption in the course of hostility that Russia displayed during the 1970s? Are we on the verge of a great change that can benefit all nations? How far will it go? No one has all the answers. It will take a few years of consistent improvements in the East-West relationship before confidence finally is felt by all parties involved. For the time being, proceeding with caution is probably the best strategy.

Indeed, there is room for optimism that these negotiations may represent the beginning of a working relationship between the East and the West that could go a long way. It could also mark the beginning of a technological exchange. The accord is a milestone toward opening closed gates and expanding international trade. In time, fruitful results ranging from cooperative research to joint ventures in space could be realized.

What will a global recession do to all those positive developments? Will it lead to acceleration of the negotiations and more decisive progress for the better? Or will it adversely affect mankind's hope of peace on earth? Nobody has a crystal ball, but we should all care about these critical questions.

THE MAN WITH THE NICE SMILE AND IRON TEETH

That was how Soviet President Andrei Gromyko described his comrade Mikhail Gorbachev when the latter assumed power in 1985. In the Soviet Union, it is customary for leaders—especially the man who holds the position of General Secretary—to remain on the political scene for a long time. Considering Gorbachev's positive initiatives, it pays for us to examine the man and assess his trustworthiness, which lies at the heart of future relations.

He is described as charismatic, charming, persuasive, and a head of state par excellence. He left his mark in Europe and almost everywhere else he went. He is articulate and elegant and has a touch of class never before seen in Soviet leaders. Gorba-mania has touched both people and politicians. After decades of stereotypical Soviet leaders—old and threatening— Gorbachev is young, energetic, and soft spoken. He walks and behaves in a humble and peaceful manner. One has to admit that he is handling his duties with the utmost carefulness.

While he is seeking and initiating a new path for East-West relations, he refuses to acknowledge the weaknesses of socialism. He believes that socialism has conquered unemployment, homelessness, and health care problems. And he is accustomed, due to the system he was brought up in, to see the world in one color; he cannot understand the wide gap between the ghettoes and Fifth Avenue in New York City. He disapproves of Stalin's massacres in public, yet he still backs up Cuba's Castro. He is a savvy defender of his political and economic roots. Yet he is willing to compromise and to deal with other ideologies.

Gorbachev is a master communicator who has studied in depth the Western political hemisphere. He dislikes questions pertaining to lack of freedom of the press, free elections, freedom of speech, and probably freedom at large in the Soviet Union. He escapes answering questions about Afghanistan and other Soviet policies in the Eastern bloc. He also evades answering many questions that compare the two economic and political systems. He is defensive at times with news reporters and pounds on the table when asked critical questions. He is very good at evading questions raised by the media. But, for the time being at least, he is willing to talk peace, and the West doesn't mind listening.

PERESTROIKA ... RESTRUCTURING BEHIND THE IRON CURTAIN

The Union of Soviet Socialist Republics is the largest country in the world. It is also the home of socialism. Half the country lies in the permafrost zone, and the other half comprises the East European Plain. The population is very close in number to that of the United States, but the standard of living between the two peoples is not comparable. Since his appointment as General Secretary of the Communist Party, Gorbachev has consolidated his position as a Soviet leader and has embarked on major reforms, both domestic and international. His movement is called *perestroika*, which means restructuring.

Despite its great wealth of natural resources, Russia's economy has been sluggish, and growth has been difficult to achieve. The growth of the labor force has slowed down, and costs of extracting raw materials have soared. Inefficiency has been overwhelmingly cited in most major sectors. The emphasis of centralized institutions has been on quantity rather than quality, which has resulted in huge stockpiles in some products and shortages in other vital ones. Most goods are heavily subsidized, and bureaucracy is ill-equipped to deal with a complex modern economy. Labor productivity is low because of the nonexistence of incentives and chronic alcoholism, which in 1985 reached epidemic proportions. Capital formation in the Soviet Union has declined, as central planners have fostered consumption rather than investment. Equipment in the agricultural and industrial sectors has aged, and their technology has lagged far behind that of the Western nations.

One of the factors most detrimental to economic growth has been defense commitments. In 1986, defense expenditures were estimated by Lloyds at 14 percent of their net material products—much higher than that of any major industrial country.

Gorbachev's *perestroika* is targeted at revitalization of their technology and modernization of their aging factories. He has initiated healthy economic and political dialogues with European nations and the United States. His drive for the reduction of medium-range missiles has been a step forward toward opening the doors for international cooperation. He has been trying to avoid the costly rivalry of Star Wars defenses.

Perestroika has received mixed reviews by Eastern European countries. For several decades, Eastern communist countries have squelched all signs of political and economic reform. They got accustomed to the state's firm control of the political and economic process and have doubts about internationalization of trade with the rest of the world. A sudden switch from the Stalinist system of central economic planning to reforms and cooperation with the West is disorienting for them.

The Soviet Union may finally have realized that its declining technological competitiveness is hindering its progress. It is hoping for some infusion of Western know-how and advanced technology to solve its economic stagnation. It is looking forward to expanding its trade with the West.

While receptive to the idea of peace, Western investors would like assurances of access to domestic markets of the communist bloc. Joint ventures with socialist countries have thus far been met with little interest from Western entrepreneurs. The big lag of Soviet technology and their lack of modern industrial infrastructure make the process of reform proceed at a slow pace.

FROM COLD WAR TO DETENTE TO COOPERATIVE SURVIVAL

As we are entering the twenty-first century, we are faced with an explosive population in the Third World. Resources are depletable, and the pie is shrinking. No nation can bear the cost of a third world war. Even those who fantasize about the chances for a first strike should realize that it would still mean their end; technology has made it impossible for man to take that chance. The best of all hopes is that the above-mentioned strides toward peace finally bring a permanent peace. Only when this is realized can the world concentrate on the more serious challenges ahead of humanity. The world today needs to find alternative resources much more than we need to reassert ideological beliefs.

Trust will be built from years of cooperation between the superpowers. The gradual reduction of short- and medium-range missiles is a first step that leaves much to be desired. Further progress aimed at reducing long-range missiles should be the final objective of the two superpowers. Ultimately, government spending should be targeted at creating both wealth and opportunity for the people.

The future holds great promise for mankind. Peace may not be far away. Only time will tell. Optimism has to be the world's choice. The superpowers have to assume their roles in a world of savvy competition and limited resources. Instead of spending huge amounts on armaments, nations can channel these funds into cooperative research. The new wave that is bringing socialist countries closer to free enterprise is a positive step forward for humanity. It could have a significant impact on the whole world and the global economy as well.

extended, and the consumer savings rate is at its lowest level since World War II. The agricultural sector continues to struggle through a depression that started earlier this decade. Forces of disinflation are at work, and commodity prices are subdued. Third World countries are suffering from budget deficits, and payment of their debts is questionable. Meanwhile, Japan has pursued aggressive pricing strategies and has invaded the world economy on all fronts. The newly industrializing countries (NICs) are also taking their place in the international arena as potential competitors. Finally, we witnessed, in 1987, the worst single-day stock market crash in history. The only other time that a similar decline in securities values occurred was at the onset of the Great Depression of the thirties.

On the positive side, the weakness of the dollar should help our products to gain competitiveness in the world market. Moreover, we live in the age of supertechnology, which can achieve wonders for mankind. We could map out our future and target the power of technological discovery at finding alternative sources of growth. Most important, we have an entrepreneurial economy and the inner talents within our borders to find solutions to our problems.

The pressing issue we are now facing is how to manage carefully our fortunes during the critical time ahead. The crash of 1987 alerted us to our vulnerability just when we thought that things were heading for the better. Our awareness of the seriousness of the challenges we are facing today is only the first step toward acknowledging the need for action. Our next task is to examine and assess some of the options available to rectify these imbalances. Our decisions have to encompass the environment that surrounds us, both domestic and international. There is no straight and easy path out of the complexity of today's problems. And we have to move quickly to prevent these challenges from turning into a painful experience.

MISCONSTRUED BELIEFS

Many people are still highly concerned about the resurgence of inflation. Since the beginning of the eighties, the nation's attention focused on the fight against rising prices. However, in the next few years, we should be concerned about fighting deflation.

Granted, inflation has its sharp edge. It disrupts corporate planning and the entire price structure of the marketplace. It distorts accounting for pensions and retirement and eats away our savings and net worth. Yet moderate inflation is not all bad. It is an integral part of our world of supply and demand. Controlled inflation keeps people on the alert; when they become complacent, they stand to lose in terms of purchasing power.

Deflation, on the other hand, is depressionary by nature. As such, it is much more destructive. It takes our earning power away from us and opens the door to great economic calamities. Deflation creates unemployment and destroys industries and companies. We have to recognize that deflationary forces are in place today and should continue to be present well into the first half of the 1990s. Numerous factors should continue to exercise downward pressure on the overall price structure ahead, as follows:

1. The large debt incurred by the less developed countries (LDCs) should keep commodity prices subdued. Most of these countries are exporters of raw material and natural resources. Pressured to meet their hefty debt service obligations, they have to export their goods at any price.

2. The price of oil, which is controlled by OPEC, should remain contained as long as the war in the Middle East persists. The painful lessons of the energy shortage of the past have prompted consumers to conserve. North Sea oil reserves have also challenged the power of OPEC. With the exception of sporadic gains due to seasonal factors, commodity prices will suffer from infrastructural deflation for the next few years.

3. In addition to commodities, debt at the corporate and consumer levels is deflationary. To pay these debts, consumption has to be curtailed. This, in turn, will cool off demand and push prices lower. As the debt liquidation process continues, prices of goods will be subdued and profits will decline.

4. Demographic factors suggest that Western economies should remain under deflationary pressures well into the middle of the 1990s. Following the bulge of the baby boomers, the birthrate dropped substantially. Consequently, the number of new entrants into the labor force—and hence consumption—should decline in the years ahead. Also, the pressure of expanding demand in all sectors of the economy should taper off or at least stop rising.

   For example, demographic patterns suggest that no sudden or unexpected demand for real estate is likely to emerge over the next few years. This could be interpreted as deflationary, since activity in the housing market is expected to remain subdued.

5. Technology is a double-edged sword. On one hand, it opens the door to more efficient means of production. On the other, it replaces people wherever it is applied. Its capacity to create new jobs is undermined by the ever-larger numbers of workers who are displaced from the job market. The competitive world in which we live is compelling us to move aggressively toward automation. The manufacturing plant of the future will be dominated by the steel-collar workers: robots.

6. Technological discoveries are pushing us more toward the service sector. Income gains will be contained, as we have to put up with the lower wage structure of the service society. This combination of the above-mentioned technological factors and the modest compensation of the service sector suggests that deflationary pressures are imminent in the income structure for years to come. Technology is promising new horizons of abundance, yet it threatens our capacity to earn more.

7. Another factor that contributes to deflation is the globalization of the world's economy, where countries with different wage and cost structures compete. That new efficiency in the international market is compelling us to
increase our productivity and to lower the prices of our
goods. Here again, while a global economy promotes the
comparative advantage principle, it simultaneously exer-
cises a deflationary bias.

8. Monetary policies adopted by central banks in all industrialized nations, including the United States, have been
stringent for the better part of the eighties. Real interest
rates have been excessively high for many years. Under
these tight monetary policies, governments have been
exerting fiscal stimuli and have been running deficits.
These deficits are now holding interest rates from declining further. Moreover, the declining dollar has made the
Federal Reserve Board (FED) hesitant to lower interest
rates. High real interest rates are deflationary by definition.

9. Finally, the wave of deregulation that has proliferated
during the 1980s is leading to increased price competition.
Prices of goods and services have cooled off and dropped
in many industries. Not only has this happened in the
United States, but in other countries as well. In fact, the
trend toward divestiture of government-owned institutions has spread throughout all Western economies as
well as other countries around the world. The end result
has been a surge in efficiency and a decline in prices,
which further testify to the trend toward deflation in many
sectors of the world economy.

There is no doubt that we are living in a deflationary
environment that should continue and probably exacerbate
for many years to come. The world should fight the pressures
of declining prices, since they threaten the global economy
with a depression.

Instead of dwelling on the runaway inflation of the seventies and early eighties, we should ask ourselves about the
severe slowdown encountered in the agricultural sector.

What caused it? Was it a special case or was it due to declining prices? One may say that it was caused by oversupply. While this is true, we prefer to say that declining prices of agricultural products caused that calamity. In other words, deflation in the agricultural sector had evil consequences that have been hurting the farmer since the beginning of the eighties.

The economic boom in Texas has also reached a grinding halt since the price of oil plummeted. Here again, deflation in that vital commodity led to a wave of bankruptcy.

The real estate bubble is also threatening us. We should not underestimate its broad-based effects on the domestic economy. If it should burst, it will have an unequivocally deflationary impact on almost all other sectors of business. Rising unemployment could aggravate further the debt liquidation process and create a severe glut in the marketplace.

Hence, we should be more concerned with fighting deflation rather than inflation. We should always keep in mind that as bad as inflation is, it did not cause a depression in either Argentina or in any other South American nations, where inflation is double-digit. We should also realize that deflation was the main cause of the Great Depression. As a nation, we should be fighting deflation, and we may even welcome a little bit of inflation. It is much safer this way.

PLEASE DON'T CUT THE DEFICIT ... IN A HURRY

In ˜modern economics, government deficits are a fiscal policy stimulus. According to Keynesian theory, deficits are used to stimulate demand in the economy during phases of contraction in business activities. During the 1930s, Keynes attempted to convince President Roosevelt of the effectiveness of such a policy, but was met with hesitation. However, the huge government spending that accompanied World War II proved the desired effects of the fiscal policy stimulus and gave credence to the Keynesian theory.

Many people blamed the great crash of 1987 on the huge budget deficit. Voices from around the nation demanded that

Washington resolve that issue immediately. Cutting the budget deficit became the hottest topic for the media and every analyst around the nation.

However, it is inaccurate to blame the stock market decline on the budget deficit. The budget deficit has been in existence since the Dow Jones Industrial Average was below the 800 level back in 1982. From 1982 to 1987, as the budget deficit rose, so did the stock market.

In our judgment, the stock market may have looked into the valley and felt uncomfortable with the excessive bullish enthusiasm, the outrageous ratio of consumer debt to personal income, the extended speculative fever in the real estate market, the loss of manufacturing competitiveness around the country, the rising trend of imports, the international economic situation, the threat of major default of the LDCs, or any combination of these factors. It is unfair to blame it all on the budget deficit.

The stock market crash signalled the possibility of an economic recession. The future course of the market depends on the reaction of the monetary authorities and business managers. We are faced with a myriad of unresolved issues that we have to deal with as a nation. If we tackle these problems with care, the stock market does not have to fulfill the prophecy of doom of the 1930s. On the other hand, if we take the task ahead lightly, the stock market will proceed as it did in the past.

Although many are demanding that the government cut the budget deficit, isn't it true that if it were cut in a hurry, this would lead to fiscal retrenchment? Wouldn't the government stop spending on projects that employ people and afford them income? Earned wages from those projects are used to consume goods and services. *Resolving the budget would ultimately entail a slowdown in consumption demand, as a result of removal of wage and income support from many individuals. Fiscal retrenchment is recessionary, and cutting the budget deficit in a hurry is equivalent to raising interest rates.*

The budget deficit is only part of the picture. If we resolve it in a hurry, it will have a recessionary effect on the economy that could bring about a severe adjustment. Gradual resolution is much more effective if we are to hope for a soft landing.

Future policies should address the deficit as part of a much broader number of issues at hand. Revitalizing our industrial base, devising solutions to deal with excessive levels of debt and overspeculation in real estate, and fighting the deflationary structure of prices are as important as resolving the budget deficit. Granted, the deficit has caused us to become a debtor nation and has reached alarming proportions, but resolving the budget deficit without these other issues could have its own deflationary contribution to an ailing economy. Balancing it in a hurry could, indeed, have devastating repercussions.

WHY TAKE THE TAX INCENTIVE AWAY FROM THE IRA?

A few years ago, John Tempelton, one of the most successful money managers of our time, commented that he foresees a shortage in securities ahead. Back then, the incentive of the individual retirement account (IRA) was still intact, and a large number of those tax-deferred dollars were going into equities. Since its implementation in 1982, the IRA tax advantage was hailed as a source of future savings to the economy. It allowed households to defer taxes on a modest portion of their earnings and to invest them in promising vehicles with the hope of handsome appreciation over the years.

Much of the money saved in IRA accounts was channeled into buying equity securities in the open market. This provided liquidity to the economic system, so that corporations could easily raise money to meet long-term plans to reindustrialize and meet the challenges of a more competitive global economy.

The changing tax structure that went into effect in 1987 removed that incentive from the IRA investment and abolished long-term capital gains. While we now lament the historic low savings rate in the United States, and envy the Japanese for their huge savings, we have discouraged the capital formation that the IRA incentive provided. Although it is true that people can still contribute to their IRA accounts, the lack of a tax incentive to do so will hold back many investors.

Instead of fostering capital formation, we chose to encourage the pursuit of short-term gains. The result of such a policy is to increase speculation and promote consumption. Yet we need to boost our monetary reserves and work hard toward resolving our economic problems. This can only be achieved by investing for the long term and increasing the base of capital available for our companies. However, we are now denying our corporations the cash that they need to revitalize and to reindustrialize in order to improve our competitiveness abroad and to regain our market share.

Instead of devising ways to control volatility in the financial markets—which resulted from the proliferation of options, futures, and options on futures—we have taken from people a good incentive for making long-term commitments. The IRA could have provided a savings base to relieve Social Security of a heavy burden in the future, as the baby boomers reach retirement age. A secure generation in their graying years can only yield a positive outcome to both America and the overall economy.

THE ROAD BACK TO COMPETITIVENESS

What are our options if we are to avert a replay of the 1930s? What should we focus on to prevent our nation from reliving an ordeal of the dimensions of the Great Depression? Do we stand a chance for a soft landing? Today's environment is filled with uncertainties and challenges.

We are faced with rising industrializing nations around the world, which could provide quality products at reasonable prices. For a while, however, we may be spared unrelenting competition from the Japanese industrial samurai. Over the next few years, Japan may have to cope with several infrastructural problems and an unavoidable prolonged adjustment.

U.S. corporations have already started on the path back to reindustrialization. Competitiveness is rising, and the distorted perception of lack of American quality is diminishing. Quality never left the United States to begin with. We still have the most sophisticated research and development (R&D) base in the world, and expenditures on that end are on the rise. America enjoys the highest levels of innovation and entrepreneurship and is endowed with abundant natural resources and human resources.

To manage the imminent adjustment, we have to manage the debt plague that has mushroomed into the economy at all levels. The ratio of consumer debt to personal income is at its highest level since World War II. The balance sheet of corporate America is laden with debt. Credit quality in business has substantially deteriorated. Government debt is very large. We financed our deficit by relying heavily on foreign money. But we should remember that foreigners have no vested interest in the long-term prospects of America; they are here for their own profit. Our savings are inadequate to meet our investment demands. A heavy debt problem among the developing countries places U.S. banks at great risk. We have lived beyond our means and have turned into a debtor nation. We are now faced with a series of structural problems that we have to tackle with the utmost care.

Deflation is our enemy and should not be allowed to exacerbate. Unfortunately, debt liquidation is deflationary, as debt is paid off from resources that would otherwise have gone to consumption. Resolving the budget deficit is fiscal retrenchment that is also deflationary. The LDC debt is deflationary, as these nations may have to sell their commodities at any cost to pay their debts. If bankruptcy rises, especially in the banking sector, it would exercise downward pressures on prices and would be deflationary. Technology also leads to declining prices as it drives the world toward higher efficiency.

Meanwhile, interest rates are too high, which is also deflationary.

During this painful debt liquidation phase, we should keep real interest rates low. The FED has the critical task of reinflating the economy if we are to hope for a soft landing. Solving the budget deficit without a corresponding increase in the money supply could only aggravate the consequences of the debt liquidation process. Unemployment compensation could add to the deficit a burden that would be too heavy to carry. Inflation does not lead to depressions, but deflation does. Calling it "disinflation" does not negate its depressing effect, and reinflating the economy should be high on everyone's agenda.

RESPONDING TO DEFLATION

While misplaced government intervention was a burden in the seventies, the economy needs well-planned strategies for the future. The adjustment that the economy must go through during the rejuvenation process should be met with cooperation between government and business. Corporate America should move its manufacturing bases back home, since offshore operations have taken away jobs that are needed in the domestic economy. Unions seem to have learned to live with the world's competitive environment and orderly automation.

Training of displaced workers deserves the attention of management and our educational institutions. Development of technical skills should ease workers' interface with computers and the automated environment, which we cannot escape if we are to be competitive. Our universities and colleges have to restructure their curricula to emphasize science and engineering. We need more engineers in our future than we needed MBAs in the seventies. Efforts to revive R&D should proceed at a faster pace to discover new applications that can, in turn, create wealth and lead to economic growth.

Household debt should ease, as a slower economic environment develops. Foreclosures may be unavoidable. In fact, they have characterized every bubble in real estate for the past three centuries. Raising taxes on low brackets could only intensify the liquidation process, as it leads to less consumption and an inability to meet debt payments. A gradual decline of debt is a much more plausible goal. If tax legislation were to be restructured, it should be planned around fostering savings and rebuilding household liquidity. It should reinstate the long-term benefits of investing in the future of America.

Bipartisan coalitions are needed now more than ever. Republican or Democrat, we should remember that, above all, we are American. The structural problems of the global economy and the U.S. economy are not easy to resolve and require decisive action. Fiscal and monetary stimuli are one way to deal with the problems. But policies targeted toward supporting R&D and improving our educational system are no less important for long-term growth.

Choices have to be made, and decisions have to be executed. The common factor behind all calamities in the history of man is complacency. The stock market crash of 1987 should therefore be heeded well by the administrators, the Treasury, and the FED. A severe economic adjustment should be prevented at any cost, even if it means the resurgence of inflation.

WOULD THE NEXT LEE IACOCCA PLEASE STAND UP

With all the challenges we will face in the difficult years to come, we need to persevere and to team up as a nation to reinstate our industrial superiority in the world. Let us call upon the recent past, when the Chrysler Corporation was a shadow of a corporate structure amid the Japanese invasion of the auto market.

In 1980, Lee Iacocca went hat in hand to Washington to ask for a huge government loan to save Chrysler. Years of complacency in the auto industry, the oil shocks of the seventies, and the Japanese energy-efficient and competitive small cars left behind an industry in dire need of restructuring. Faced with a grim outlook, a militant union, and productivity at its all-time low, Iacocca accepted the challenge to bring back Chrysler to its past greatness. The company had been suffering from noncompetitiveness for more than a decade.

With the grace of a leader and an expert free enterpriser, Iacocca assembled a team of executives at Chrysler like a maestro picking members of a concert band. Iacocca hired Dick Dauch, a capable manufacturing executive from Volkswagen, in 1980. Dauch's management style was more inclined to motivating, introducing improvement, and dealing with marginal producers with an iron fist. Together, Iacocca, Dauch, and the rest of the team at Chrysler started by addressing customers' needs. Quality was the ultimate objective of all decisions. Then they attacked the issue of product diversification to meet a broad variety of market tastes.

All this restructuring was further enhanced by effective and well-thought-out marketing and advertising campaigns of the new Chrysler Corporation. They featured the commanding statement, "If you find a better car, buy it."

Their next target was the modernization of the antiquated facilities that they had inherited. Spinning off manufacturing facilities that did not fit the new competitive age of the automobile industry was a major undertaking. Automation was introduced slowly at first—and then on a large scale.

The result was a clean and mean company that won the consumer's attention. Chrysler's New Yorker, Fifth Avenue, and LeBaron GTs are among the best cars produced by the auto industry in the 1980s. It is a story of success. An entrepreneur at heart, Iacocca took Chrysler back to profitability and beat the Japanese at their own game. The legendary comeback of Chrysler is living proof that American companies can compete and regain their long-lost international status if they have the discipline, the commitment, and the will to survive and accept the challenge.

Let the Lee Iacoccas come to the forefront of corporate America and lead the way toward revitalization of our industries. Let us make quality our top priority and plan as if tomorrow matters. There are many Lee Iacoccas within the ranks of the system, who are capable of reinstating our manufacturing leadership and bringing us back to the glory of the post-World War II era, when "Made in America" reflected a people's pride.

THE BILL GATESES OF AMERICA

In 1975, William H. Gates III founded Microsoft Corporation, a major producer of software for personal computers, when he was still in his teens. In 1986, at the age of 31, he went public and amassed a fortune that placed him among the richest people in the United States. His company set standards for personal computers, the PC-DOS and the MS-DOS, which led to millions of IBM PCs and clones. Gates is only one example of the entrepreneurship that exists and is nurtured in the United States.

Our past and present are full of names of entrepreneurs who, in pursuit of self-actualization, built great industries and revolutionized the world. Andrew Carnegie, the founder of U.S. Steel, believed in keeping pace with economic growth during good times and expanding aggressively during periods of economic contraction. Henry Ford left his mark on modern and future manufacturing by mechanizing the process of producing goods for the masses. He was a century ahead of his time. An Wang, a Chinese immigrant, is an engineer who applied the science he learned in America to revolutionize the office with his tiny thinking machines. Sam Walton, the founder of Wal-Mart Corporation, brought name-brand merchandise to small town America and made his mark among the giants. In the early 1960s, Ken Olsen, the founder of Digital Equipment Corporation, started his company with $77,000 in venture capital. He brought the mainframe computer down to a cheaper price, which makes it affordable for smaller corporations.

Only in America! Imagine if Gates, Wang, Walton, Olsen, or even Ford had been born elsewhere in the world. They might have succeeded, given their creative spirit and know-how. But only in the homeland of free enterprise could the best of their achievements come to the forefront to serve mankind.

Every age has its pioneers. At times, circumstances may play a role, and the hand of destiny may have its final say. Yet one should always try and persevere. It is through the spirit of entrepreneurship, which does not yield to the power of the unknown, that nations can overcome what others may consider an inescapable script. Yes, the real estate market may be vulnerable. Yes, our industrial base needs to be revitalized. Yes, our competitiveness has to be boosted. But it is within our control to steer out of our difficulties and to emerge triumphant as we always have. Meeting the challenge of adversities and scoring against all odds have been an integral part of our history and should remain alive for future generations.

At this stage, we need the creative spirit that helped us to achieve our technological and institutional gains. The responsibility vested upon us, as leaders of the free world, should prompt us to devise solutions to pull us—and our world—out of the problems that lie ahead. There are many Gateses, Olsens, Fords, and Watsons in America, and now is the time for them to live up to their responsibility to the future.

THE COMING INDUSTRIAL RENAISSANCE

In boxing, experts say that the comeback knockout is the most sensational of them all. The pendulum has now gone too far, and it is time to change direction. Fortunately, we are endowed with the richest natural resources on the face of the earth. The baby boomers are entering the years of their peak productivity, peak innovation, and peak achievement. We have the most highly skilled labor force in the world. We have the most sophisticated industrial infrastructure. We have the most advanced laboratories in the West. We conquered space, and we emerged from the Great Depression to lead the world toward the new frontiers of supertechnology. We have many Henry Fords, Thomas Watsons, Ken Olsens, Graham Bells, and Bill Gateses in America. We can persevere and prevail. We can regain our lost industrial and manufacturing superiority.

But the coming industrial renaissance demands hard work. Corporations, people, and the government have to recognize the urgency of proceeding forward with firm plans to reverse the trend of our declining standard of living. Productivity has to rise and an honest dollar for an honest day's work has to come back. We have to invest more in our future. Technology today creates opportunities, but only for those who are willing to invest in mastering it. The world ahead of us demands higher skills, solid education, and superior knowledge. These can only be attained if we restructure our curricula to meet the challenge of our fast-moving technology.

We also have to train displaced workers to cope with the automated factory of tomorrow, and we have to arm ourselves with the technical and scientific knowledge that will be needed. We have to invest in basic research to look for answers to economic stagnation, and we have to formulate policies to protect our findings from being given free to our competitors. We have to continue our research in space, which may hold the answers to many of our problems today. We have to rethink our unilateral trade policies with foreign countries that refuse us access to their markets. We have to adopt policies that protect promising industries from foreign invaders who steal our innovations and sell them back to us. We have to plan for the coming labor shortage, as the baby boomers move into their graying years.

On a personal level, we have to stop living beyond our means and seriously face the challenges ahead of us. We also have to save more, as savings allow for future investment. We have lived for the past two decades in a consumption-

driven economy, whereas the Japanese have lived in a sav-
ings-propelled society. We became debtors, and they became
creditors. It is time to rethink our savings and investment
habits if we hope to see our standard of living rise again.

All these challenges are on the list of things we have to
deal with in the future.

THE NEXT CIVILIZATION ...
SEEDS OF AMERICA'S GREATNESS

Sluggish economic growth, declining competitiveness in
the international arena, and deteriorating productivity over
the past two decades have led to the perception that the
United States is losing ground in world affairs. Intellectuals
say that America's economic and institutional structure is
following closely the pattern that the United Kingdom followed at the turn of the century. They predict that our standard of living will recede and that we will be unable to preserve our leadership of the Western world. They even suggest
that Japan is ready to assume that superpower position and fill
the gap that the United States is leaving behind.

We admit that there is sense to that logic, as no nation
has ever had sole claim to civilization. Empires have come,
prospered, and gone. Who would have thought that the
home of the great Roman Empire would end up in the economic disarray that Italy has been in for the past few decades?
Who would have imagined that Egypt, host of the oldest civilization known to man, would become a Third World country? Where have the Ottomans, the Phoenicians, and the
massive empire of Alexander the Great vanished? Thinking
along these lines shows us what history holds for people and
nations.

However, history is not destiny. If we first explain why
civilizations flourish in certain countries, at particular times
in history, we can then examine some of the pertinent facts
behind the decline of the British Empire, the rise of the
United States, and the potential of Japan.

Civilizations that dominated before the industrial revolution were mainly based on military might, strong leadership, superior organization within the leading governing body, and cultural sophistication. With the advent of the industrial revolution, the size and efficient usage of land, labor, capital, and technology played an important role in shaping the economic and political power of nations.

First, land and the richness of natural resources have always been major determinants of the strength or weakness of nations since the early days of man's life on earth. While land maintained its importance for many past civilizations, it is unable to explain the failure of Africa, with its abundant resources, to assert itself as a world leader. The largest two nations in the world are Russia and Canada, yet the standard of living of both countries trails that of the United States. Moreover, South American nations are blessed with ample resources, yet they have been unable to live up to their potential. Instead, they continue to focus on ideological differences and political beliefs. The United Kingdom, the empire where the sun never set, has until early in this century benefited from the extensive resources it had. However, the loss of its protectorates and colonies after World War II deprived its economy of many rich resources.

On the other hand, Japan has proved until now that it could dominate the international trading arena and grow despite its lack of natural resources. Its technology, skilled labor, and institutional structure compensated for its limited land and poor resources. Japan proves that technology can compensate for the other economic determinants of national growth. However, for those betting on Japan, we remind them that the rise of the industrial samurai as an economic superpower could not have materialized without access to the vast American market. U.S. willingness to open its market to Japan, an ally, created the Japanese legend.

There is no doubt that among the leading industrial nations in the world, the United States is blessed with vast land and ample natural resources. While Japan badly relies on imports to supplement its poor agricultural base, the United

States has a rich agricultural sector that could literally feed the world.

Second, today, one should consider not only the sheer number of people in the labor force, but also the level of their skill and education. Here, again, the United States has the most highly skilled labor force on the face of the earth. The Japanese have not in 30 years pioneered any scientific breakthroughs; they merely copy the technology from American laboratories.

Third, the capital base in the United States is the most highly advanced in the world. Silicon Valley is a symbol of the technology of tomorrow. The transistor was discovered at Bell Laboratories. Then there was large-scale integration. Later, the microprocessors, the mainframe, the mini, and the personal computers were developed. Japan has proven over and over to be a copy machine of the superior technology produced in America. Their robots were originally licensed by Unimation Corporation, and their microprocessors originated in the labs of Texas Instruments, Motorola, and IBM.

Fourth, scientific discoveries picked up speed. Technology, as a matter of fact, has helped the West to leap forward into the future. What was a luxury in the past has become a necessity in our lives. Consider the electric light bulb, the telephone, the automobile, the airplane, the air conditioner, the radio, the television, and the computer. During the past 100 years, the world has progressed at a logarithmic speed never before imagined in the history of mankind. Technology grew to be the most important determinant of economic achievement.

Two additional factors have emerged as preconditions to industrial maturity. The size and breadth of the marketplace in a country supports or denies the degree of its institutional and technological effectiveness. And the institutional structure of a country determines the efficiency of the use of technology. If we are to speculate on the home of the next great civilization, we ought to assess the future in terms of land, labor, capital, technology, market size and breadth, and institutional structure.

The market breadth of the United States cannot be matched by that of any other country in the world today. As far as institutional structure, the United States has the most flexible and effective framework in the world. Just think how resilient the economy of the seventies was to absorb masses of new entrants into the labor force! Also, education plays a greater role in our society today. Management science and business administration techniques have replaced the entrepreneurial knack of business founders with professionally run organizations. Today, the institutional structure determines the strategies that are most efficient at utilizing all available factors of growth and maximizing shareholders' equities. Multinationals and giant corporations have benefited from management disciplines that have tamed economies of scale to generate profits and to give jobs to the masses. Again, the United States has excelled in this field.

Considering all these factors, the characteristics of Japan and the United States bear no similarities to the developments that preceded the great transition of leadership from the United Kingdom to the United States. In sum, the next Great Civilization will still find its home in America long after we are gone.

TALES OF THE TEA LEAVES ... THE STOCK MARKET

The stock market represents the sum total of the opinions of all participants—with all their knowledge and ignorance—about the future course of the economy. It has long been recognized as the leading barometer about phases of contraction or expansion in business activities. The FED keeps track of stock market action and incorporates this information into the 12 leading indicators that have long been used to formulate future monetary policies. Markets have accurately predicted past calamities and prosperity long before they became apparent in economic statistics.

Where is the stock market going? When asked about the future direction of the stock market, Bernard Baruch once said, "It will fluctuate." Generally, bull markets follow bear markets, and good times are followed by bad times.

The crash of 1987 was severe in both magnitude and intensity. It shook the world and awoke us to our vulnerability to a bleak future if our complacency continues. It sounded an alarm and screamed foul about the fundamental structures in which we are living. It delivered a message that could hardly be ignored by those who have studied past market history. Wall Street professionals took it as a prophecy of doom. The whole investment community panicked, and business sections of major newspapers recounted economic calamities that were predicted by the equities markets.

During the great bull market of 1982–1987, the investment community became enthusiastic about the predictions of wave theories. We were told that the world is governed by waves over which we have no control. Because of the accuracy of the predictions of the analysts who attributed their brilliance to the wave theory, we began to believe in the theory rather than in the capability of those analysts. It is hard for us to believe that corporate finance, market strategies, the global economy, competitiveness, technological evolutions, and monetary and fiscal policies are governed by predestined waves. We *can* control the shape of things to come. The stock market is simply an assessment of how well we are doing.

Over the next few years, the stock market will tell us how we are faring in our drive to deal with our future challenges. If we continue to be haunted by inflation and we do not fight the pressures of deflation and falling prices, the stock market will continue to plummet. More important, if we do not tackle our competitiveness in the global economy and reestablish our industrial might, the stock market will continue to slide. If we do not plan for the development of new technologies and proceed with serious R&D, the stock market will continue to warn us of doom.

The prophecy of the tea leaves should continue to play the role it has always played in our future. The stock market is an accurate barometer that we must watch closely so that we can act quickly to rectify inefficiencies and to resolve imbalances.

BUY AMERICAN

American companies are still the world's best examples of quality and innovation. Hewlett Packard, IBM, DuPont, Exxon, Ford, and many others have stood the test of time and are leaders in their businesses. Their quality standards have always been beyond the shadow of a doubt. Unfortunately, the auto industry suffered amid the economic environment of the 1970s. The success of the industrial samurai in this field was mainly due to his price competitiveness and market share strategy, which he implemented with the utmost care. The oil shocks helped him to get a well-deserved break; the American automakers were taken by surprise and had little time to react.

Fascination with foreign quality led to a major shift in perception of our own products. Should we really continue to follow the fad of buying imports and leave it up to someone else to buy what we produce, from which we derive our living? Why buy the Mercedes and BMW while, if you can afford it, the Lincoln Continental, the Cadillac, and the other lines of American-made luxury cars are available. Today, General Motors, Ford, and Chrysler have proven to the world that they can revitalize and that American know-how can rejuvenate itself. They are setting the record straight worldwide.

The state of our trade imbalance has reached alarming proportions that threaten the existence of our manufacturing base. We do not have to look to our administrators in Washington to impose protectionism; our share of help should be the starting point. At this critical and sensitive juncture of our economic history, we should realize that every contribution makes a difference. We have a unique set of price structures in our domestic economy and we abide by stringent gauges to measure our companies' profitability, yet we are not willing to consume our own products and give our earned money to our own companies. How can needed cash flow be obtained without consumption expenditures within the borders of our own country?

As consumers, we should consider that each time we buy foreign products, we are making it difficult for our companies to get the resources to plan, produce, and give us jobs. Commenting on the closed market in Japan, a Japanese executive said that their consumers return products that do not carry the label "Made in Japan." Meanwhile, our fascination with the foreign-made label has exported jobs abroad and has limited our chances to stand up and compete. Unless we deal with that reality, jobs are going to continue to migrate to some other land in a remote part of the world. Our technologies will be cheaply exported to other nations that probably will not even care about supporting our cause. Our R&D base will erode, and our jobs will disappear. We may not realize that our actions make a difference. Yet they do matter in the end.

It is time to reflect on these issues and control our own destiny for a change. Every dollar that leaves our shores goes toward building someone else's fortunes and robs our corporations of a precious contribution to designing, innovating, financing, planning, and creating new jobs for the domestic economy. Consciousness of the implications of the buy-foreign attitude, which has impacted each and every corner of our industrial base, should be the backbone of our decisions in the years to come.

Do we always have to look to Uncle Sam to mind the shop? Can't *we the people* do what we have to do to help our nation to regain its industrial superiority? Granted *we the consumers* have the ultimate choice of buying the most competitive product in the marketplace. But shouldn't we stop and ask ourselves if the money we pay will help Americans keep their jobs? If we sincerely want to build a greater America, we should renew our love for and pride in "Made in America."

OUR WORLD SHOULD KNOW NO BOUNDARY

In the recent past, we may have lost a battle or two in the international trading arena. We experimented with the great service society of tomorrow, and we are now beginning to realize that we cannot do away with manufacturing. In the future, it may change to a more progressive, highly automated form, but we know that it has to stay within our borders if we are not to lose control over our strategic resources. While the great, efficient service society will continue to expand the wealth of our nation, revitalization of our industrial base is a prime concern in the years to come.

Progress is cumulative in nature, and long-term goals are the solution to all the misfortunes of the past. The world will never end its waves of adjustment and change. Every time mankind thinks that the ultimate success is within reach, nature's laws are quick to remind us of our vulnerability. However, we emerged triumphant from the devastation of the Great Depression, which left behind a generation of American warriors who brought victory home. This triumph was not only realized in World War II, but in the scientific, economic, social, and political revolution that we brought to the world. It was because of that bruised generation—children of the great ordeal—that the standard of living of the average American rose far above that of any other country in the world.

This generation is no less prepared to meet the challenges ahead. It serves nobody's interests to dwell on the great achievements of the past or to yield to complacency in the future. There is no heroism in predicting the disasters of the next great depression; rather, we should meet adversity with resolve. Perseverance has been the hidden source of every success story in the history of mankind and will continue to be the source of progress for the remainder of man's life on earth. This generation is you and me and he and she. It is our responsibility to add to the gains that we inherited through the evolution of technological, institutional, and ideological processes.

As we look at the number of challenges that our world faces in the space age ahead, it should serve us well to remember the words of John F. Kennedy:

And so my fellow Americans: Ask not what your country can do for you—ask what you can do for your country. My fellow citizens of the world: Ask not what America will do for you, but what together we can do for the freedom of man.

WE LOOK FORWARD TO AN AMERICA ...

We look forward to an America that commands respect from the rest of the world, not because of our sheer military power but because of our civilization.

We look forward to an America that carries high the banner of freedom and steers the spirit of free enterprise toward fulfillment of its promise to mankind.

We look forward to an America that leads the world into ever-growing prosperity in the twenty-first century.

We look forward to an America that continues to fulfill its promise to the needy and the homeless.

We look forward to an America that encourages entrepreneurs to carry their innovations to new frontiers that will solve the future problems of the human race.

References, Bibliography, and Supplemental Readings

We owe a great deal to the information society and more to the excellence of our communications media. We are blessed with the efficient and timely reporting of developments around the world. Our magazines and educational institutions have been doing a great job of keeping us abreast of the changes taking place around us. Without that wealth of information, we may not have been able to fully conduct this study. In the following pages, we provide you with a list of great articles on this subject. We believe that reading the full articles sheds greater light on the topic. The order of the magazines or institutions has no bearing on the importance or excellence of the work done. Again, we owe our thanks to these institutions for enlightening us about the world in which we live.

HARVARD BUSINESS REVIEW

Ballantine, Arthur A. "When All the Banks Closed." March 1948.

Bower, Joseph L., and Eric A. Rhenman. "Benevolent Cartels." July-August 1985.

Crane, Dwight, and Samuel L. Hayes III. "The New Competition in World Banking." July-August 1982.

Davidson, William H., and Phillippe Haspeslagh. "Shaping a Global Product Organization." July-August 1982.

Ellsworth, Richard R. "Capital Markets and Competitive Decline." September-October 1985.

Gerwin, Donald. "Do's and Don't's of Computerized Manufacturing." March-April 1982.

Hamel, Gary, and C. K. Prahalad. "Do You Really Have a Global Strategy?" July-August 1985.

Hayes, Robert. "Why Japanese Factories Work." July-August 1981.

Heskett, James L. "Lessons in the Service Sector." March-April 1987.

Johnston, George S. "Dr. Kaufman's Guide for the Perplexed." November-December 1986.

Kaplan, Roger. "Entrepreneurship Reconsidered: The Antimanagement Bias." May-June 1987.

Killing, J. Peter. "How to Make a Global Joint Venture Work." May-June 1982.

Kiser, John W. "Tapping Eastern Bloc Technology." March-April 1982.

Kizilos, Tolly. "Krattylus Automates His Urnworks." May-June 1984.

Levinson, Marc. "Asking for Protection Is Asking for Trouble." July-August 1987.

Levitt, Theodore. "The Industrialization of Service." September-October 1976.

Podhoretz, Norman. "The New Defenders of Capitalism." March-April 1981.

Quinn, James B., and Christopher E. Gagnon. "Will Service Follow Manufacturing into Decline?" November-December 1986.

Redford, Robert. "Search for the Common Ground." May-June 1987.

Reich, Robert B. "Entrepreneurship Reconsidered: The Team As a Hero." May-June 1987.

Sibbernsen, Richard D. "What Arbitrators Think About Technology Replacing Labor." March-April 1986.

Sutton, Charlotte D., and Kris K. Moore. "Executive Women—20 Years Later." September-October 1985.

Vlachoustsicos, Charalambos A. "Where the Ruble Stops in Soviet Trade." September-October 1986.

Wack, Pierre. "Scenarios: Uncharted Waters Ahead." September-October 1985.

Weiss, Andrew. "Simple Truths of Japanese Manufacturing." July-August 1982.

Wellons, Philip. "International Bankers: Size up your Competitors." November-December 1982.

Wheelwright, Steven C. "Japan: Where Operations Really Are Strategic." July-August 1981.

Young, Harrison. "Bank Regulation Ain't Broke." September-October 1986.

Zuboff, Shoshana. "New Worlds of Computer-Mediated Work." September-October 1982.

BUSINESS WEEK

"America's Quest Can't Be Half-Hearted." June 8, 1987.

Baker, Stephen, Steven J. Dryden, and Elizabeth Weiner. "A Whiff of Hope for Ravaged Central America." December 21, 1987.

Bartlett, Sarah. "Are Banks Obsolete?" April 6, 1987.

Bernstein, Aaron, et al. "The Difference Japanese Management Makes." July 14, 1986.

Buell, Barbara, and Steven J. Dryden. "Strong, Silent Japan Starts to Speak Up." November 30, 1987.

Byrne, John A. "At Sanyo's Arkansas Plant the Magic Isn't Working." July 14, 1986.

"Chase's Battle to Catch Up." April 9, 1984.

Field, Ann, and Catherine L. Harris. "The Information Business." August 25, 1986.

Hall, Alan, Cahan, Vicky, et al. "The Race for Miracle Drugs." July 22, 1985.

Holstein, William J. "Japan, U.S.A." July 14, 1986.

"How an LDC Default Would Hit the U.S. Economy." November 7, 1983.

"How to Cut the Deficit." March 26, 1984.

Mervosh, Edward, et al. "Living with Disinflation." July 15, 1985.

Norman, James, et al. "America's Deflation Belt—Falling Commodity Prices Are Turning the Heartland into a Wasteland." June 6, 1986.

Pennar, Karen. "Is Credit a Go-Go Headed for a Grinding Halt?" November 18, 1985.

Pennar, Karen. "Is the Financial System Short-Sighted?" March 3, 1986.

Pennar, Karen. "The '20s and the '80s: Can Deflation Turn into Depression?" June 9, 1986.

Pennar, Karen, and Edward Mervosh. "Women at Work." January 28, 1985.

Port, Otis. "High Tech to the Rescue." June 16, 1986.

Port, Otis. "The Push for Quality." June 8, 1987.

Shulman, Roger, et al. "The Gene Doctors." November 18, 1985.

Smith, Emily T., and Jo Ellen Davis. "Our Life Has Changed." April 6, 1987.

"The New Shape of Banking." June 18, 1984.

"The Peril of Financial Services." August 20, 1984.

Wallace, G. David, et al. "America's Leanest and Meanest." October 5, 1987.

Weiss, Andrew. "Simple Truths of Japanese Manufacturing." July-August 1984.

"Will Mexico Make It?" October 1, 1984.

Wilson, John W., and Judith H. Dobrzynski. "And Now, the Post Industrial Corporation." March 3, 1986.

Wolman, Karen, and Elizabeth Weiner. "Computers: The New Look." November 30, 1987.

FORTUNE MAGAZINE

Bylinsky, Gene. "America's Best-Managed Factories." May 28, 1984.

Bylinsky, Gene. "The High Tech Race—Who's Ahead?" October 13, 1986.

Fierman, Jaclyn. "John Reed's Bold Stroke." June 22, 1987.

Hector, Gary. "Third World Debt: The Bomb Is Defused." February 18, 1985.

Mayer, Martin. "Coming Fast: Services Through the TV Set." November 14, 1983.

Norton, Robert E. "The Dollar: How Low Should It Go?" December 7, 1987.

Rowan, Roy. "How Harvard's Women MBAs Are Managing." July 11, 1983.

FORBES

Michaels, James W., William Baldwin, and Lawrence Minard. "Echoes from a Siberian Prison Camp." November 9, 1981.

Wriston, Walter. "A New Kind of Free Speech." December 14, 1987.

SRI INTERNATIONAL—BUSINESS REPORT PROGRAM

Allen, Dot. "The promise of home information services." Research Report No. 682, Summer 1983.

Everett, Sidney J. "The environment: A continuing business challenge." Report No. 736, Summer 1986.

Hampden-Turner, Charles, and Franklin Carlile. "Lifestyle Marketing: Scenarios of satisfaction." Report No. 743, Winter 1986–1987.

Jacobson, Kenneth H. "Regional conflict in the 1980s." Report No. 701, Spring 1984.

Royce, William S. "Challenges to management, 1984." Research Report No. 692, Winter 1983–1984.

Schmidt, Klaus D. "Business customs and protocol in the Asian Region—Part 1." Report No. 720, Summer 1985.

Shorney, Cindy, and Alan Purchase. "Computer-aided publishing: The new office revolution." Report No. 746, Winter 1986–1987.

Starry, Claire. "Consumer spending in the United States." Research Report No. 685, Summer 1983.

Trondsen, Eilif. "Changing perspectives on protectionism." Research Report No. 683, Summer 1983.

Wachter, G. Thomas. "Global strategies in manufacturing industries." Report No. 727, Winter 1985–1986.

THE CONFERENCE BOARD AND ACROSS THE BOARD

Brown, James K., and Evelyn Samore, eds. "Getting More out of R&D and Technology." The Conference Board, Research Report No. 904, 1987.

Collins, Lora S. "The U.S. Economy 1990." The Conference Board, Report No. 864, 1985.

Deudney, Daniel. "Coming Down to Earth—Industry in Space Is a Mirage of Abundance." Across the Board (November 1982).

Fritz, David. "FDIC to the Rescue." Across the Board (May 1983).

Graham, Margaret B. W. "R&D—Lessons from America's Great Experiment." Across the Board (May 1987).

Gregg, Gail. "Woman Entrepreneurs: The Second Generation." Across the Board (January 1985).

Hein, John. "A New Protectionism Rises to Fight Free Trade." Across the Board (April 1983).

Hein, John. "What Will the GATT Beget?" Across the Board (September 1985).

Kranzberg, Melvin. "Invention Is Mother of, Well, More Invention." Across the Board (May 1987).

Markman, Steven. "1916—The Year of Living Dangerously." Across the Board (May 1986).

Mellow, Craig. "By Debt Possessed." Across the Board (January 1985).

Pinchot, Gifford. "Promoting Free Intraprise." Across the Board (March 1985).

Reeves, Richard. "An American Tocqueville in the USSR." Across the Board (May 1983).

Rogers, James T. "The Information Revolution in Space." Across the Board (May 1983).

Smith, George D. "Why Companies Can't Afford to Ignore the Past." Across the Board (May 1986).

Thurow, Lester. "White-Collar Overhead." Across the Board (November 1986).

FEDERAL RESERVE BULLETIN

Burns, Arthur F. "The Anguish of Central Banking." September 1987.

Savage, Donald T., and Elaine J. Peterson. "Interstate Banking Developments." February 1987.

Wilson, John, et al. "Major Borrowing and Lending Trends in the U.S. Economy, 1981–1985." August 1986.

U.S. DEPARTMENT OF COMMERCE—
"FOREIGN ECONOMIC TRENDS" AND
THEIR IMPLICATIONS FOR THE UNITED STATES

American Embassy in Beijing. "People's Republic of China." September 1987.

American Embassy in Moscow. "USSR." December 1985.

OTHER MAGAZINES/JOURNALS

"A Blueprint for Upgrading Foreign Aid." *Japan Update*, Keizai Koho Center, Japan Institute for Social and Economic Affairs 43 (August 1987).

Baily, Martin N. "Productivity in a Changing World." *The Brookings Bulletin* (Summer 1981).

"Banker of the Year—John Reed of Citicorp." *Institutional Investor* (September 1987).

"Banks Will Have to Accept Larger Third World Debt." *Financial Times* (September 28, 1987).

Breneman, David W. "The Humanities in a Technological Society." *The Brookings Bulletin* (Spring 1980).

Cato, Ralph. "How Today's 'Gurus' See the K-Wave Theory." *Futures* (May 1986).

Corwin, Philip S. "A Banker's Guide to the Moratorium." *ABA Banking Journal* (October 1987).

"Gov't Pressed for Action to Buoy Ailing Economy." *The Japan Times* (February 25, 1987).

International Commercial Bank of China. "Ninth Medium-Term Economic Development Plan for Taiwan (1986–1989)." *Economic Review* (March-April 1987).

"Japan as a Suitable Leader." *Financial Times* (September 28, 1987).

"Japan—Economic Report 1986." *Lloyds Bank.*

Jo, Toshio. "Furnaces Extinguished As Demand for Steel Cools." *The Japan Times* (February 21, 1987).

Kotkin, Joel, and Yoriko Kishimoto. "Theory F." *Inc.* (April 1986).

Masaki, Hisane. "Jobs Are Lost As Shipbuilders Cut Capacity." *The Japan Times* (February 20, 1987).

Miyagawa, Kyoihi. "The Final Blow to Japan's Failing Textile Industry." *The Japan Times* (February 22, 1987).

Okada, Keisuke. "Export Leaders Face Loss of Competitiveness." *The Japan Times* (February 24, 1987).

"Price Stabilizing Effects of the Yen's Appreciation and Influence on Enterprises and Households." *The Bank of Japan,* Special Paper No. 150, April 1987.

"Reaching for an Understanding." *Japan Update* (Keizai Koho Center, Japan Institute for Social and Economic Affairs) 3 (Winter 1987).

"Restructuring of Economy Promises to Be Painful." *The Japan Times* (February 26, 1987).

"Rising World Protectionism." *The Bank Credit Analyst* (December 1986).

Saito, Kakeshi. "Further Weakness of the Dollar Should Be Avoided." *Fuji Bank Bulletin, Ltd.* (July-August 1987).

Stocken, Dick. "Are We Riding a Kondratieff Down Wave?" *Futures* (August 1986).

"The Banking System: Sowing the Seeds for the Next Crisis." *The Bank Credit Analyst* (April 1986).

"The Coming Financial Mania." *The Bank Credit Analyst* (March 1986).

Tsumura, Tsuneo. "The Clouded Job Picture in Japan." *Japan Update* (Keizai Koho Center, Japan Institute for Social and Economic Affairs) 5 (Autumn 1987).

"With a Nudge from Endaka, Japanese Producers Head for Foreign Shores." *Japan Update* (Keizai Koho Center, Japan Institute for Social and Economic Affairs) 5 (Autumn 1987).

BOOKS

Brooks, John. *Once in Golconda, a True Drama of Wall Street 1920–1938.* W. W. Norton & Company, 1969.

Drucker, Peter. *Innovation and Entrepreneurship.* New York: Harper & Row Publishers, 1985.

Editors of *The Economist. The New Deal—An Analysis and Appraisal.* New York, 1937.

Galbraith, John Kenneth. *The Great Crash 1929.* Boston: Houghton Mifflin Company, 1961 edition.

Goldston, Robert. *The Great Depression.* New York: Fawcett Premier Books, 1968.

Hoover, Herbert. *The Memoirs of Herbert Hoover, The Great Depression 1929–1941.* New York: The Macmillan Company, 1952.

Kristol, Irving. *Two Cheers for Capitalism.* New York: Basic Books, 1978.

Levien, J. R. *Anatomy of a Crash—1929.* New York: Traders Press, 1966.

Peters, Thomas J. and Robert H. Waterman, Jr. *In Search of Excellence.* New York: Harper & Row Publishers, 1982.

Rothbard, Murray N. *America's Great Depression.* New Jersey: D. Van Nostrand Company, Inc., 1963.

Schultz, Harry D. *Panics & Crashes.* Westport, Conn.: Arlington House, 1980.

Schumpeter, Joseph A. *Capitalism, Socialism and Democracy.* New York: Harper & Row Publishers, 1942.

Shannon, David A., ed. *The Great Depression.* Englewood Cliffs, N. J.: Prentice-Hall, 1960.

Shuman, James B., and David Roseneau. *The Kondratieff Wave.* New York: Dell Publishing Co., Inc., 1972.

Simon, William E. *A Time for Truth.* New York: Reader's Digest Press, 1979.

Werstein, Irving. *A Nation Fights Back.* New York: Julian Messner, Inc., 1962.

Index